Data Base
Computers

Lexington Books Series in Computer Science

Kenneth J. Thurber, General Editor

Data Base Computers

Olin H. Bray
Harvey A. Freeman
Sperry Univac

LexingtonBooks
D.C. Heath and Company
Lexington, Massachusetts
Toronto

Library of Congress Cataloging in Publication Data

Bray, Olin H.
  Data base computers.

  Bibliography: p.
  Includes index.
  1. Data base management. 2. Electronic digital computers. I. Free-
man, Harvey A., joint author. II. Title.
QA76.9.D3B7   001.6'4   78–24765
ISBN 0–669–02834–7

Copyright © 1979 by D.C. Heath and Company.

Second printing, May 1979.

Published simultaneously in Canada.

Printed in the United States of America.

International Standard Book Number: 0–669–02834–7

Library of Congress Catalog Card Number: 78–24765

Contents

              Comparisons   150

Chapter 6   **Conclusions**   155

              Architecture Trends   157
              Data Management Trends   159

              Bibliography   163

              Index   177

              About the Authors   180

List of Figures

List of Tables

Foreword

The presence of the book by Olin H. Bray and Harvey A. Freeman marks an important turning point in the annals of computing. The point signifies the departure of traditional emphasis on nonnumeric processing of data by general-purpose mainframes and the arrival of innovative solutions to non-numeric processing of data by special-purpose backends. One of the most important backends is the data base computer. This machine is intended to cost-effectively replace the conventional data base management software, on-line I/O routines, and on-line secondary storage (currently supported by the general-purpose mainframe) while offering better performance.

The timely arrival of data base computers is prompted by a number of factors: the user's application requirement for very large data bases and for a wide range of data base activities, the enhancement of existing and the configuration of new technologies, the performance bottlenecks of the present-day software-laden data base management system, the lack of reliable and secure software solutions to data base management, and better research and understanding of hardware approaches to data base computer architecture. Bray and Freeman have skillfully articulated these factors.

More important, these two talented authors attempt to review the data base computer architecture work to date, classify the various architectures, and compare the different approaches to data base computer architecture. Such a review, classification, and comparison, although difficult to develop, provides the reader a much-needed perspective and understanding of the field of data base computer architecture.

Finally, the authors are congratulated for their concluding remarks about the trend of data base management and the future of data base computers. As practicing computer architects, they should be taken seriously on their views of the upcoming data base management software and hardware evolution.

Since this is the first book written on data base computers, it should be required reading for every serious computer science and engineering practitioner.

David K. Hsiao
The Ohio State University

Preface

Data base computers, first proposed by researchers in various universities in the early 1970s, are now being developed by commercial computer manufacturers. Within the next few years, these special-purpose devices will be available to meet the information storage and processing needs of the 1980s. Which designs will actually be implemented and which ones will achieve a measure of success is not clear at present. What we can say at this time is that we expect a wide variety of data base computers to be offered, with attractive features and capabilities.

This book was written to familiarize the reader with data base management requirements and data base computer concepts. Until now, no systematic means have been available for comparing and evaluating current or future data base computer designs. This book will be useful to designers in their efforts to achieve the benefits attributed to these special-purpose machines. It also provides future purchasers and users of data base computers with the ability to specify the features and capabilities required for their applications and the knowledge to use them effectively. Finally, this book will extend the vision of computer science and engineering students and practitioners in yet another area of the exciting technological realm of the computer.

We thank George Champine and Ken Thurber of Sperry Univac and David Hsiao of The Ohio State University for their help and encouragement in writing this book. The assistance of Jayanta Banerjee, who contributed the CODASYL DMS comparison of chapter 4 and reviewed our manuscript, is greatly appreciated. We also thank Jerry Bill who reviewed our manuscript and Jan Bray who assisted with the Index. Special thanks are due to Linda Sorenson and Penny Svenkeson who contributed their data entry and text editing skills as our deadline rapidly approached.

1 Introduction

Data base management systems (DBMS) development is facing a challenge to its continued growth and effectiveness. As the variety of functions of DBMSs increases, so does the accompanying overhead. Critical response time and the throughput requirements are not met because of the implementation of DBMSs on unsuitable architectures. A way must be found to reduce this overhead, increase the performance of data management systems, and allow more of the processing power of computer systems to be used in the applications.

The challenge stems from the incompatability between traditional computer hardware architecture and the functional requirements of data base management. General-purpose computers locate data (whether stored in main memory or on secondary storage devices) by position or address, whereas most data management applications employ data by content or value. Significant processing and storage overhead is necessary, therefore, to convert from one reference scheme to another. This overhead can become so extreme that in some data bases the indexes and tables to locate the data require more storage than the data itself.

Since the early 1970s, at least eight universities (Ohio State, Toronto, Syracuse, Florida, Texas, Utah, MIT, and Kansas State) have initiated research projects to address this challenge. The results of this research are now being used by various computer manufacturers to develop commercial products in this area. In October 1977, International Computers Limited (ICL) "announced" CAFS (Content Addressable File Store),[1] which is similar to some of the work done on CASSM (Context Addressed Segment Sequential Memory) at the University of Florida.[2] The University of Toronto's RAP (Relational Associative Processor) project has designed and built a prototype relational architecture which Intel considered implementing.[3] Syracuse University and the Rome Air Development Center are jointly investigating the applicability of STARAN, Goodyear Aerospace's associative processor,[4] for data base management applications.[5] Sperry Univac is working closely with David Hsiao at The Ohio State University in exploring the commercial viability of his DBC (Data Base Computer).[6]

The use of back-end data base computers is similar to the use of front-end message processors. As users required increasingly complex and sophisticated communications and message processing capabilities, these functions were distributed to a specially designed, separate processor. Data base systems are now approaching a comparable stage of development. The use of DBMSs has become widespread enough to consider the possible effi-

ciencies and performance improvements of distributing the data base
management function to separate specialized devices or computers.

As with message processing, some of the early work with data base
computers, such as Canaday's at Bell Labs, proposed the use of general-
purpose processors as the backend.[7] However, new technologies such as
microprocessors, VLSI, charge-coupled devices, and magnetic bubble
memories, incorporated in special-purpose data base computers (DBC) in
conjunction with such design approaches as content addressing and parallel
processing, appear better suited to the information storage and processing
needs of the 1980s.

Although it is assumed that the reader is familiar with data base concepts, this first chapter provides a brief review. The data management trend
of providing greater funtionality in the system software to relieve the application programmer of the routine data management burden is discussed.
Also identified are the basic data base management objectives. Then the
components and operation of a DBMS are described. This concludes with a
treatment of the data base computer concept. The concept of the DBC is
described, several classifications are noted, and the advantages and disadvantages of the DBC approach are discussed.

Chapter 2 identifies the requirements of DBMSs. These requirements
exist regardless of the way the system is implemented. Three types of
requirements—basic, extended, and future—are identified. The basic ones,
such as retrieval, update, control, and data administration, are already
available in most current DBMSs and therefore must be available in any
commercial DBC system. Extended requirements are those which are just
being introduced in the more advanced DBMSs. Future requirements cover
those which are rarely available today, but which are anticipated to become
widespread in the future. These include data compression, encryption, and
value-based security criteria.

Chapter 3 describes the example data base which will be used as a
means for comparing the various DBC architectures. The example is a
production data base for a typical manufacturing application. The set of
queries to be processed against the data base is identified, and three data
base structures are shown. The first structure is the conventional
CODASYL or network structure. Because many DBC architectures are
oriented toward the relational model, however, the second and third structures are relational. The second structure is a relational data base as it
would be designed given the set of queries to be used. The third alternative
is the relational data base that would be obtained using a conversion algorithm to convert the data base from the network to the relational model.

The fourth chapter provides a set of criteria against which to evaluate
various DBC architectures. These criteria include performance, cost, range,
and evolvability.

Chapter 5 first provides a way of classifying various DBC architectures based on where the data base is searched and on the number of processors involved. Then the benefits and problems of each of the resulting major architectural types are discussed. All the current DBC systems are located within this framework. Finally, a representative example of each type is examined in detail. This includes a description of both the hardware and the way the system would process the example data base described in chapter 3.

Chapter 6 draws some conclusions and makes some projections about future developments in the DBC area. Both data management and system architecture, that is, hardware and software, trends are identified.

Following chapter 6 is a bibliography for those individuals who would like further information about the concepts and systems treated in this book. This bibliography is divided into the major categories of data base management systems, data base computers, and miscellaneous items. These major categories are further divided to assist the reader in locating references to a particular topic.

1-1. Data Base Systems

In data management the basic trend is to relieve the programmer of most of the routine aspects of data management. In the early 1950s, the programmer had to do all of his own I/O, and at a very low level. The actual application and how the data were to be used was only a part of his concern. Much of the I/O programming involved testing the status of the I/O device, readying the device, issuing the appropriate operations (which were different for different types of devices), waiting for the device to complete the operations, rechecking the device status, and perhaps redoing the entire sequence if there was an error. Only at this point could the programmer be sure the data had been properly read or written.

Much of this activity, however, was of no interest to the applications programmer, who simply wanted to read or write a block of data and to be notified if there was a problem. Also much of this programming was determined by the I/O device being used, rather than by the nature of the data. Because these functions were the same for all applications using a particular type of device, computer manufacturers began supplying them in the form of a common set of software. These early IOCSs (input–output control systems) relieved the programmer of the routine burden of directly managing the computer hardware. Application programmers could concentrate on the application, while a few knowledgeable systems programmers could develop I/O routines to make the most efficient use of these specific devices. While these improvements were important for first- and second-generation systems, they were critical for third-generation systems where multiple users are processed concurrently during each other's I/O wait times. I/O, which had been both an application and a system bottleneck, was now primarily an application bottleneck because multiprogramming and time-sharing systems allowed the system to make more effective use of the I/O wait times. All these improvements were in the use of hardware and were independent of the data content and organization.

A similar trend occurred for data content. The applications programmer knew the form of the data as they came from the devices and the form in which they were needed by the application. Therefore, he or she converted the data before they were used. If the file containing the data base was labeled, the label had to be processed differently from the data in the file. If the tape was blocked, it had to be deblocked and individual records passed to the application. Thus label processing and blocking and buffering were absorbed in the vendor-provided software and became a system rather than an application programmer concern.

Sorting and merging of files also occurred frequently enough that most computer manufacturers and many independent software houses provided standard SORT/MERGE packages which the programmer could use by specifying only a few parameters.

Because many files were being written and read by programs written in high-level languages such as FORTRAN and COBOL, data fields required certain standard conversions. In FORTRAN, these conversions are specified in the format statements. In COBOL, the data division provides this data conversion and structure information. While the applications programmer had to know the format of the file and had to specify which conversions were required, he or she was not concerned with how the conversions were done. These routine operations also were performed by the system software.

Thus the basic trend was that as common data manipulation requirements were identified, system software routines and utilities were developed. Programmers then performed these functions simply by specifying a few required parameters rather than by writing the entire program.

Even the most sophisticated file system, however, has very little information about the content of the file it is processing. The development of file systems proceeded using a bottom-up approach: "Here is a function being done by many applications. Can that function be more effectively provided by system software?" Instead of reexamining the overall requirements of application development, the designers of these data management systems accepted the file approach as given. Certain basic characteristics of file systems, however, limited their ability to continue to relieve the applications programmer of additional data management functions.

There are three basic characteristics of file processing. First, a file is designed for a specific application. It is used by only a few programs, frequently one to create or update the file and one to read and process it. This application-specific design leads to the second characteristic of file processing. The definition of the file's logical (and much of its physical) structure and content is implicit in the program using it. Therefore, the program must know the file's data structure and format. Finally, because the file system knows little or nothing about the file's content, it can provide only basic data management support for the applications programmer. Because of these characteristics, file systems allow only a few simple organizational structures, that is, sequential, indexed sequential, and random.

These file-processing characteristics create three major problems: integrity, consistency, and maintainability. The integrity problem arises because the file system does not know enough about the file to automatically check the validity of the data being entered.

The consistency and maintainability problems arise because there are cases where the same data may be needed by several applications. For example, the cost of an item in inventory is needed for inventory management, accounts/payable, and for reporting profit margins by item. When this overlap occurs, the systems analyst has two options. One is that two or more files can be used, although the supposedly common data, for example, the cost of the item, may not agree. This is particularly true if the files are updated at different times. This creates the consistency problem. The same data item has a different value depending on the file from which it was read. When this inconsistency becomes apparent to the user, the information system loses its credibility.

This inconsistency can be avoided by combining the files into a single file which contains the data needed by all the applications. This creates a maintenance problem. When one of the programs is modified and needs additional data, the file must be changed. The other programs which use the file, however, make certain assumptions about its structure. Therefore, when the file is changed to meet the new needs of the first program, the other programs also will have to be changed so that they can continue to use the file. Thus there is a tradeoff between consistency and maintainability of the data. Data base management (software) systems were developed to eliminate or ease these problems.

1-2. Data Base Management Systems

Objectives

The basic objective of any data base management system (DBMS) is to improve an organization's control and utilization of its data resources. This is accomplished through improvements in the availability, integrity, and security of the data base. These are basic data management objectives and are applicable regardless of whether or not there is a data base computer (hardware) system.

The first data base objective, availability, has three components, the first of which is ease of use. The easier it is to learn the system and access the data, the more the system will be used, particularly by the nonprogramming user.

The second component involves allowing multiple users to access the data simultaneously. Certain controls must be provided, however, to prevent destructive interference caused by multiple users trying to concurrently update the same data. The performance aspects of multiple–user availability are response time and throughput. If the response time and throughput are degraded too much, the result is that the data are not available.

The third availability component is long–term availability or evolvability. This means that the data base and the DBMS must be flexible so that they can evolve to meet changing user needs. This evolvability requires a generalized rather than a specialized system and a programming language interface so that system modifications can be made as new requirements are identified.

The second requirement for a DBMS is improved data integrity. Data integrity in turn has two components: data quality and data existence. Data quality first requires providing a complete definition of the data base so that the DBMS can perform much of the validity checking automatically. Anything that has been specified previously in the data definition or schema can be checked and maintained by the system. Second, data quality requires access control to prevent multiple users from concurrently updating the same part of the data base and destroying its accuracy.

Integrity also involves the existence of the data base. This protection requires appropriate backup and recovery methods. The recovery methods must allow for both a complete or partial loss of the data base and an erroneous entry. The latter situation is made more difficult because an incorrect entry may not be detected for some time, during which its effects are propogated to other parts of the data base. Recovery must then correct both the original and all subsequent errors.

The third objective of DBMSs involves the security or privacy aspects of the data base. Because a firm's data resources are an invaluable asset, unauthorized personnel should not be allowed access to it. Thus a second type of access control that the DBMS must provide becomes apparent.

If the data base contains information of a personal nature, there is also a question of privacy. The person(s) involved as the object of these data should have some control over its distribution and use. Access to the data must be limited to the authorized purposes. Although this area has frequently been ignored in the past, privacy legislation in both the United States and Europe is making this a growing concern.

Tradeoffs must be made among these DBMS objectives. The essential tradeoff, however, is between performance and the functions provided. With regard to performance, response time and throughput are the critical aspects. The system must meet the users' needs in both these areas. Functions, in this context, include availability, integrity, data security, and privacy. Unfortunately, these functions are obtained only at the expense of performance. For example, with data independence, the DBMS automatically translates the data from their stored form to the form expected by the user. This makes the system easier to use, and the data base can be restructured without program modification. This automatic data translation, however, requires additional processing time and storage. Therefore, both response time and throughput are affected. From another perspective, though, this performance versus functional tradeoff is simply the question of machine versus people efficiency.

There are several related trends in the data processing industry affecting the development of DBMSs. These trends impact both the user and the vendor. The first factor is the scarcity of manpower. There are not enough trained personnel available to design and develop new applications. This problem is even more acute because the same personnel pool also must be used to maintain current operational systems. In many cases these systems use the older file systems. These initial attempts at managing the data are expensive and time consuming to maintain, partly because of the way they were designed, but primarily because of their inherent lack of user support. DBMSs now are widely used to reduce these development and maintenance problems. Their high-level query languages allow quicker development, particularly in those cases where the end-user can generate his or her own query without the assistance of a programmer. In addition, applications developed using high-level query languages tend to be simplier and therefore easier to maintain. The data independence provided through automatic mapping between schema and subschema also eases the development effort and eliminates much of the maintenance problem. Thus the DBMS approach improves personnel efficiency but requires a more general and flexible system that is less efficient on current computer hardware. Considering the cost trends for personnel and hardware, however, this seems to be an appropriate tradeoff. Hardware, including processors, main memory, and secondary storage, is becoming less expensive and more powerful at the same time. Personnel costs, however, are rapidly increasing, while the people themselves are only marginally more productive. These divergent trends are shown graphically in figure 1-1. The tradeoff of machine efficiency for personnel efficiency applies equally well to both computer users and computer manufacturers.

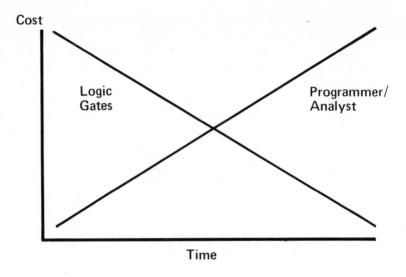

Figure 1-1. Divergent Cost Trends of Hardware and Personnel.

Components

Given the previously stated objectives of a DBMS, this section describes the basic components of a data base management system and explains their operation. As with the objectives, these components are in current DBMSs and also will be in future systems, including those installed on data base computers.

Data base management systems (DBMSs) consist of four basic parts:

1. A schema or data base definition.
2. The data base itself.
3. The subschema or user–schema.
4. The DBMS procedures.

Because these components include much more information about the structure and content of the data than file systems, the DBMS can provide much greater support for the applications programmer.

The schema, the first component, provides a complete logical and physical definition of the data base. This information has been removed from and exists independently of the various application programs using the data base. Information on the data structure and content can now be used by the DBMS to provide additional support to the user as well as to the applications programmer.

The logical definition includes both the structural and content information. It specifies the real-world entities (for example, customers, parts, orders, bills, invoices, and suppliers) described by the data base. A definition of the data items describes or identifies each entity or record type. A description of the various ways in which the entities can be related also is present. At the data item or content level, the schema indicates data item name, size, the type of values it can assume, and the range or set of valid values. This allows the DBMS to check the validity of new or changed values.

The physical or storage definition describes the way the data base is actually stored. This includes the data item size and its possible encoding. Also specified are record sizes, record clustering, record placement, and record location information. For example, a set of related records may be stored in physically contiguous locations, linked by pointers embedded within the records, or linked through a pointer array or an inversion table. The appropriate method is determined by how the data base is used and not by its logical structure, or by anything directly specified by the users. The physical definition also specifies the size of the physical storage blocks, how to handle storage area overflows, and various device-dependent characteristics. These factors are determined primarily through performance requirements. Therefore, any changes in the physical structure of the data base should be transparent to the user, except to the extent that the system's performance is seriously affected.

The second DBMS component is the data base itself. The data base is the largest unit of data recognized and managed by the DBMS. Different DBMSs are predicated on different data models which constrain the logical structure of the data base. Both the data definition and the data manipulation languages are partly dependent on the data model underlying the DBMS. The simplest data bases contain a single record type with no internal logical structure. Slightly more complex systems allow repeating groups within the single record type. These two relatively simple data base structures are primarily associated with very limited retrieval systems instead of fullfledged DBMSs.

Most DBMSs involve multiple record types and sets of relationships among them. In hierarchical data bases, a record may have multiple "dependents," but only one "parent."[8] The more complex CODASYL or network-based structure relaxes this constraint and allows multiple "parents."[9] In both the hierarchical and network systems, though, different types of records are currently linked by pointers which are either embedded within the records or in separate pointer arrays. The newer relational data model allows greater flexibility in relating various record types even though it is simpler internally.[10] This is due to linking the records by the contents of any fields within them rather than through only a limited set of predefined pointers.

The third component is the subschema. While there is only a single schema for the entire data base to describe how it is structured and stored, each application has its own subschema. The subschema describes that part of the data base which the application uses and defines the structure and format of the data as the application sees them. The subschema contains much the same information as the schema, except for the physical storage definition, which is transparent to the user. If the DBMS does not include the concept of a subschema, the user must be aware of the entire data base and must accept the data in their stored form. The main constraint on the subschema is that it must be possible for the DBMS to map and convert data from the description provided in the schema to the one provided by the subschema. The effect of the subschema is twofold. First, it simplifies application development because the user only needs to describe how he or she expects the data to appear. The conversion routines are included within the DBMS and the conversion itself is done automatically. Second, the subschema provides a degree of data independence that reduces both the frequency and amount of application conversion required when the data base is modified.

The fourth component in the DBMS is the various procedures and routines which provide the basic data management functions. Examples of these functions include checking to ensure that a user is authorized to access or modify the requested data, physically locating data which the user has referenced by content, locking data to prevent concurrent updates, automatically relating various record types, checking data entering the data base to ensure their validity, and automatically converting the data between their stored form and the forms different users expect.

An important point is that only the DBMS directly interacts with the data base and its definition. The application programs cannot directly access the data base. They can only issue requests to the DBMS, which has the prerogative of rejecting a request if, for example, it would result in integrity or security violations.

Operations

This section illustrates how the various DBMS components are used in data base retrieval and update. Figure 1-2 shows the steps in a retrieval. A similar figure can be drawn for an update. However, the update discussion simply identifies how it differs from the retrieval operation.

The first step in processing a retrieval in response to a user request is to ensure that it is valid and has all the information required by the DBMS. The next step is to check the user authorization to ensure that the user is allowed to retrieve the requested part of the data base. Different DBMSs

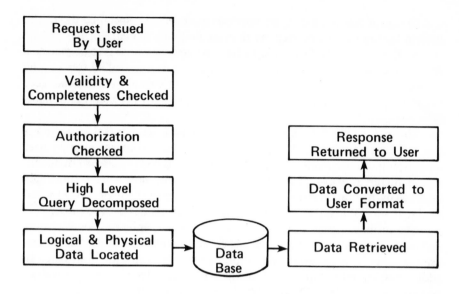

Figure 1-2. Steps in a DBMS Retrieval.

provide different levels of access control. At one extreme are those where the user, allowed to access any part of the data base, can access the entire data base. At the other extreme are those where the user's access can be restricted to certain record types or even to certain items within a record type. Some DBMSs also separate access controls by operation, so that, for example, many users may be allowed to retrieve certain data while only a few are authorized to update them.

In some cases, complex high-level queries must be decomposed into their basic components for processing. For example, some queries with complex selection expressions require several additional retrievals just to resolve the selection expression. This is all performed at the time the DBMS selects the appropriate strategy to fulfill the request. The next step, then, is to locate the data within the appropriate logical structure. This generates a logical address, that is, the unique internal record identifier or data base key, of the requested data. This logical address is then converted into an actual physical address. Given this physical storage address, the device on which the data are stored is positioned and the data are transferred into one of the DBMSs buffers. Finally, the DBMS uses the schema and the sub-schema to convert the data from the form in which they are stored to the form which the user expects. Only at this point are the converted data moved to the user's buffer and made available for processing.

The procedures followed to update the data base in response to a request are similar. The request is checked for validity and completeness and to ensure that the user is authorized to modify the specified data. The data to be modified or deleted are then located and locked. For the case of an item to be inserted, the location where the new data item is to be placed is determined. The item is then converted from the user-specified form to the form in which it is to be stored. Finally, the data base is actually changed, the lock is released, and the user is informed that his or her modification has been completed.

The major difference between the update and the retrieval operation is that the data item being changed must be locked to prevent another user from trying to concurrently update it. Different DBMSs perform this locking in different ways. The locking information, however, is normally included in the tables used to locate the data either in the logical or physical data structure. When the update is completed, the lock is then released.

The problems that occur with file processing, integrity, consistency, and maintainability have been reduced or eliminated because the DBMS can use the schema to do extensive validity checking before data storage. In addition, with only a single copy of the data, consistency problems cannot occur. The maintainability problem is avoided by having the DBMS map the data from their stored form to the user form before the user ever sees them. Obviously, there will still be certain cases where the application program will have to be modified when the data base is modified, but if the data base is initially designed properly, such cases should be relatively rare.

1-3. Data Base Computers

Concepts

The basic concept of the data base computer (DBC) is to remove all or part of the DBMS from the host and put it on a back-end system. In principle, this back-end DBC may be either a general-purpose, for example, a mini-computer, or a special-purpose computer designed specifically for data base management. In fact, for those approaches which off-load only a few functions, the DBC is usually only a subsystem rather than a complete computer system.

In this book, the term *data base computer* (DBC) is used instead of the more common *data base processor* (DBP) because more than just a processor is involved. Modified mass storage devices and controllers, parallel processing elements, and memory devices may all be included in what is actually a computer system for data management. *Data base processor* will still be used occasionally, though, since most people in this field are more familiar with this particular term.

There are several ways to classify DBCs. One classification, proposed by Rosenthal and discussed in the following paragraphs, is by the number of functions that are off-loaded from the host. Other ways, described in chapter 5, include whether or not the data base is searched directly or indirectly and whether or not parallel processing is used.

In an ideal DBMS application, the user issues a high-level request which the DBMS interprets; the DBMS also determines if the user has the proper authorization. If so, the DBMS performs a second set of operations to locate the data and perform the specified task. The way of designing a functionally distributed data base system is to draw a line through these two sets of DBMS operations and allocate those above the line to the host and those below the line to the DBP.

Rosenthal proposed a three-way classification of data base processors: (1) a smart peripheral, (2) a network node, and (3) a host-DBP configuration.[11] In Rosenthal's classification (figure 1-3), the major architectural distinction is whether the implementation is on a general-purpose processor or a special-purpose associative processor. One common assumption is that DBMS functions are I/O bound and therefore could be performed on a less powerful processor, for example, a minicomputer, more efficiently than by a large general-purpose host. In many commercial applications, however, the data base operations constitute the bulk of the processing with only a few relatively simple operations on the retrieved data. This is particularly true with those DBMSs using high-level query languages rather than record-at-a-time data manipulation languages. In general, the associative approach frequently provides much greater performance benefits. The functional distribution questions, the benefits, and the problems are essentially the same, though, regardless of the implementation.

The smart peripheral approach simply moves some of the data access and management functions from the host or mainframe into the controller. At lower levels this may include error detection and correction, device positioning, and the scheduling of the physical I/O operations. At higher levels

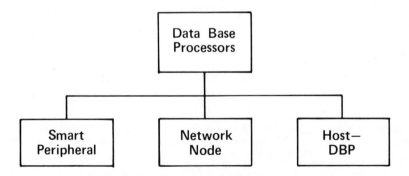

Figure 1-3. Data Base Processor Classification.

it includes associative addressing such as in CASSM[12] and RAP[13] and may even include certain relational operations, for example, selection, projection, and join. Special–purpose hardware is required for this type of DBP, which is connected to the host through an I/O channel. All the smart peripheral or intelligent controller approaches attack the basic position versus content addressing incompatability by using some form of associative processing.

Associative processing allows data to be addressed and searched by content or value rather than by physical address. All associative systems contain the same basic five elements, which are shown in figure 1–4. As shown, the data register contains the value for the search. The mask register

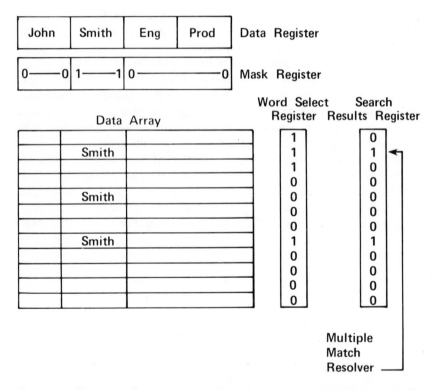

Source: O. Bray and K.J. Thurber, "What's Happening with Data Base Processors?" *Datamation* 25, No. 1, January 1979. Reprinted with permission of *Datamation Magazine*. Copyright 1978 by Technical Publishing Company, A Division of Dun–Donnelley Publishing Corporation, A Dun & Bradstreet Company. All rights reserved.

Figure 1–4. Basic Elements of an Associative System.

indicates what part of the data register is to be used in the search. The data array contains the data to be searched, although the entire data array frequently does not have to be searched. In this case, the word–select register indicates which words in the array are to be checked. A bit is set in the search results register corresponding to every word for which there was a match. When there is more than one match, the multiple match resolver (MMR) points to the first word that was found.

The network node involves a data node in a network, for example, the DATACOMPUTER developed by CCA.[14] In this case, the DBP functions as a special–purpose data management node for the entire network. This functional specialization could be provided by either a general–purpose or special–purpose processor. The essential ingredient of this approach is that the DBP is an equal node in the network. It is loosely coupled via some communications system to several, perhaps different, host systems.

In the host–DBP approach, there is relatively tight coupling between the host and the DBP. This is essentially a master–slave configuration in which the DBP fulfills the data requrests passed to it from the host. The DBP can reject requests, however, which do not conform to the DBMS access controls. The connection between the host and the DBP is usually through an I/O channel, while the DBP itself may or may not be a special–purpose processor. A summary of the characteristics of the host–DBP configuration as well as the other two categories is given in table 1–1.

Table 1–1
Summary of Characteristics of DBP Types

Factor	Smart Peripheral	Network Node	Host–DBP
Hardware	Special purpose	General or special purpose	General or special purpose
Coupling	Memory or tight I/O channel	Loose/ communication lines	I/O channel
Autonomy	DBP as slave	DBP as equal	DBP as slave
Hosts	One	Many, same, or different	Many, same, or different
Response time	Fast	Slow	Medium
Functions to DBP	Few	All	Few to all

Source: O.Bray and K.J. Thurber, "What's Happening with Data Base Processing?" *Datamation* 25, No. 1, January 1979. Reprinted with permission of *Datamation Magazine*. Copyright 1978 by Technical Publishing Company. All rights reserved.

Advantages and Disadvantages

A data base computer offers a number of potential benefits. First, there are various cost/performance benefits which may be realized through specialization, performance tuning, and the reduction in the need for and complexity of conversion. A second set of benefits include improved data base integrity and security. These benefits are only potential, however, because specific implementations and their tradeoffs determine which benefits are realized and which are sacrificed for other objectives. Similarly, there are potential drawbacks and problems. including the added costs and reliability of a second machine, multiple vendors, the potential for unbalanced resources, and the potential for performance degradation with certain applications. These drawbacks, unlike the benefits, are independent of the way the DBC is implemented. In general, though, the advantages far outweigh the drawbacks.

The prime benefit of a data base computer is performance. This is obtained through parallel processing, associative addressing, dedicated hardware, faster components, and other techniques applied to the data base management task. Performance is improved by reducing the volume of data that must be moved between the host and the data storage devices. This is accomplished by selection, projection, and data compression or encoding. Using selection, the DBC sends only those records actually needed by the application program. In a typical case in today's standard DBMSs, a thousand records may be read to find the few that answer the user's query. Projection can be used to reduce the data volume for those cases where only a few fields in the record are needed. In this case, the DBC selects only the desired records and then extracts (projects) and converts only the required fields.

By off-loading part of the processing from the host to the DBC, additional processing time and memory on the host is released and can be used by the application programs. This benefit alone can be critical if the host is approaching saturation. By off-loading the data base management functions and allowing the application programs to interface with the data base at a high level, however, the application programmer's task is simplified. This simplification and reduction of program complexity has several benefits. Because the total application is simpler and shorter, it can be designed, developed, and made operational sooner and at a lower cost. In addition, the greater simplicity of the program means less maintenance time and costs during the life of the program. Since most of the I/O interrupts and their handling occur on the DBC, the interrupt handling overhead on the host is reduced. This can provide major savings because state changes on the host can be very time consuming.

Specialization also provides certain benefits in the hardware area. If special-purpose hardware is used for the DBC, certain features and their corresponding costs are eliminated. For example, a DBC does not need such features as fast multiply and divide logic, floating-point hardware, and the long-word-size registers necessary to obtain high precision in complex arithmetic calculations. It does, however, need a powerful set of byte manipulation instructions and a high-speed I/O capability to a wide variety of storage devices.

Many of the functional benefits of the DBC occur because of the off-loading. These benefits exist regardless of whether the DBC is implemented on general- or special-purpose hardware, although special-purpose hardware normally produces much greater performance benefits. These common functional benefits include minimizing conversion problems, allowing multiple hosts to interface with a single data base, reducing the volume of data through the system, and improving the integrity, security, and backup and recovery of the overall system. Each of these benefits is discussed later.

Conversion problems can be reduced by either delaying the conversion, that is, prolonging the life of the current system, or making the conversion easier when it does occur. A DBC can extend the useful life of a system which is becoming saturated. With a DBC, a limited set of the supporting software, that is, the data base management system, is off-loaded and converted to new hardware. Most of the remaining supporting software and the applications do not need any conversion. From the perspective of applications, the DBMS has not changed if the program interface remains the same. The DBC can relieve bottlenecks caused by processor speed, memory capacity, and/or secondary storage capacity.

On the other hand, for those systems which already include a DBC, replacement of the host because of system-overload problems is much easier. Because the DBC, the link between the applications and the data base, is not changing, the actual stored form of the data does not have to be changed. That is, no data conversion is necessary. Moreover, if the applications now interact with the data base through a high-level interface, they are easier to convert.

The difficulties of data sharing among multiple hosts are also alleviated with a data base computer. Once the data base and the corresponding DBMS are on the data base computer, the data base can then be made available to other types of processors by providing an interface so that the new host can communicate with and receive data from the DBC. This is a much simpler task than modifying the entire DBMS or developing methods to allow two independent DBMSs to concurrently access the same data base.

Another DBC benefit is the improvement of the integrity and security of the data base. Because both are related to access control, integrity and security are considered together. A DBC provides a single access path to the data base. If the data base devices are connected only to the DBC, then any operation on the data base must go through the DBC. This was

Canaday's approach of using the host to issue high-level commands to the DBC.[15] The DBC then performs all the necessary data base processing to construct the response for the host. The assumption made in this case is that the DBC is a system resource and therefore is not programmable by the application programmers. This effectively isolates the application and the host from the data base and thus increases its integrity and security.

Improved backup and recovery is another possible benefit of a DBC. With a separate host and DBC, the two machines can provide a check on each other. In fact, Canaday proposes two separate logs for recovery.[16] In one, the host records all transactions or requests sent to the DBC. Thus if the DBC fails, the data base can be restored using this log. Similarly, the DBC would keep a record of all changes to the data base. If the host fails, then the recovery can be performed using the DBC's log. In each case, the recovery is done with an audit trail from the machine that did not fail in order to minimize the chance that the audit trail was contaminated. Moreover, by having one processor check on the other, failures can be detected sooner. Thus there will be less chance of the resulting errors being propogated to other parts of the data base.

There are several potential drawbacks to a DBC. These include the cost of another machine, multivendor coordination, reliability, obsolescence of the DBC, and performance degradation.

Because the DBC approach requires another machine in the system, the user incurs the cost of a second machine. However, the DBC provides additional processing power for the added costs, and the real measure should be cost/performance improvement.

Multiprocessors have traditionally meant increased reliability, because one processor could function independently if another failed. This is not true with a DBC system because both the host and the DBC are needed. For this reason, a fault-tolerant DBC is essential, especially for those cases where the DBC provides the only path to the data base. A failure of the DBC should result in graceful degradation rather than a catastrophic failure. Another approach is to provide a path for the host to bypass the DBC and get to the data base directly, although this reduces the DBC's integrity and security advantages. It also may have a relatively high cost for the vendor because a complete DMS is needed on the host for use only as a backup to the DBC.

If the host and the DBC are not provided by the same vendor, the user may face serious coordination problems. The hardware and software interfaces between the host and the DBC must be standardized, and future revisions by both vendors must conform to this standard. This can be especially critical with future software releases. In addition, ambiguous failures, those which cannot be clearly attributed to either the host or the DBC, could pose serious problems and might require cooperation between vendors in order to solve.

Another potential trouble spot might occur when the DBC becomes obsolete or saturated and must be replaced or upgraded. Even in this case, however, the problem is less serious than having to convert the entire system, because the host does not need to be converted. Obviously, the conversion is easier if there is a family of host and DBC systems through which the user can progress.

The size of the host and the DBC is determined by projecting the load on the system. When part of the system is functionally dedicated, as with the DBC, the sizing problem is more critical because resources cannot be freely shifted. For example, the overall system may have excess capacity. If the excess is all in the host and the DBC is saturated, there is no way to fully utilize the system's capacity. A similar problem would occur with mass storage devices if they were also dedicated. In general, if the system load grows in an unanticipated way, the host–DBC system might become unbalanced.

Although in most cases the DBC improves data base management system performance, there are some instances where a DBC can actually degrade the overall system performance. A minimum of two messages are required for the host to pass a request to the DBC and to obtain a response. If the performance of the DBC does not at least cover this additional overhead, there will be a performance decline. If the DBC cannot select a set of records to be sent to the host, select parts of the record, perform encoding or decoding, or reduce the number of interrupts on the host, then the performance may be degraded. Applications where a record must be examined to decide which record to process next are particularly sensitive to this kind of degradation. In many cases, however, this problem is caused by the limitations of the query language rather than by the inherent nature of the application.

In summary, the cost/performance benefits of a DBC and the increased functional capabilities that it may offer are its prime advantages. The DBC can be used to extend the useful life of an existing general–purpose host and to reduce the costs and complexity of the conversion when the host is replaced. Finally, a DBC makes it easier and cheaper to integrate a heterogeneous network into an existing data base system. Potential drawbacks include the requirement for a second machine with its additional cost, reliability, and multivendor coordination. There are also potential problems with DBC obsolescence, unbalanced loads, and performance degradation.

Notes

1. "ICL First With DB Processor," *Computer Weekly,* No. 573, October 27, 1977, p. 1.

2. S.Y.W. Su and G.J. Lipovski, "CASSM: A Cellular System for Very Large Data Bases," *Proceedings of the International Conference on Very Large Data Bases,* September 1975, pp. 456–472.

3. E.A. Ozkarahan, S.A. Schuster, and K.C. Smith, "RAP—An Associative Processor for Data Base Management," *AFIPS Conference Proceedings* 44, June 1975, pp. 379–388.

4. K.J. Thurber and L.D. Wald, "Associative and Parallel Processors," *Computing Surveys* 7, No. 4, December 1975, pp. 215–255.

5. P.B. Berra, "Data Base Machines," *ACM Special Interest Group on Information Retrieval Publication Newsletter [SIGIR]* 12, No. 3, Winter 1977, pp. 4–22.

6. J. Banerjee, D.K. Hsiao, and K. Kannan, "DBC—A Database Computer for Very Large Databases," IEEE *Transactions on Computers* C-28, No. 6, June 1979, pp. 414–429; G.A. Champine, "Trends in Data Base Processor Architecture," *Compcon '79 Spring Digest of Papers,* February 1979, pp. 69–71.

7. R.W. Canaday et al., "Back-end Computer for Data Base Management," *Communications of the ACM* 17, No. 10, October 1974, pp. 575–582.

8. IBM, *IMS/VS Programmer's Reference and Operator's Manual,* SH20-9047-0, April 1975.

9. Sperry Univac, *Data Management System [DMS 1100],* UP7907 Rev. 3, 1977.

10. E.F. Codd, "A Relational Model of Data for Large Shared Data Banks," *Communications of the ACM* 13, No. 6, June 1970, pp. 377–387.

11. R.S. Rosenthal, "The Data Management Machine, A Classification," *Proceedings ACM SIGIR-SIGARCH-SIGMOD Third Workshop on Computer Architecture for Non-Numeric Processing,* May 1977, pp. 35–39.

12. Su and Lipovski, "CASSM."

13. Ozkarahan et al., "RAP."

14. T. Marill and D. Stern, "The Datacomputer—A Network Data Utility," *AFIPS Conference Proceedings* 44, 1975 NCC, June 1975, pp. 388–395.

15. R.W. Canaday et al., "Back-End Computer."

16. Ibid.

2

Data Base System Requirements

The functional requirements of a data base management system must be identified to ensure that current and future needs are considered in any data base computer design. Requirements listed in this chapter apply to data base management systems in general. Which functions are actually implemented in the data base computer and which in the host or other system elements depend on a number of factors.

Prime among these factors is cost/performance. The data base computer must provide either improved cost/performance or greater performance than is currently available at any price. Use of parallel processing elements, content addressable memories, and microprocessors in the DBC will yield improved cost/performance for many of the identified functions. Some of the remaining functions might have to wait for such technology developements as faster microprocessors or larger and less expensive memory chips.

Another factor may be the size and type of the user's environment. One of the goals of a computer manufacturer is to develop a family of data base computers that can cover a broad range from small to large user. In this case, more functions may be implemented on the host at the low end of the series than at the high end. In addition, it may be possible to design the data base computer such that many of the functions are modularized. Then those functions which are heavily used by a particular user would be placed in the DBC and those functions which are rarely needed would be left on the host or other system elements.

The following sections describe the functional requirements of a data base computer. Section 2-1 applies to user/application-type functions. The subsection entitled "Inquiry" deals with the functions necessary to obtain selected information from the data base. The subsection entitled "Updating" describes those requirements which involve updating the data base. Conditions limiting inquiry or updating the data base by content or by position are discussed in the subsection entitled "Qualification." Included are both simple expressions and complex ones consisting of strings of qualifiers.

Section 2-2 applies to the data base management system type functions. The subsection entitled "Control" describes the requirements that allow for secure, reliable, and efficient data base operation. The subsection entitled "Data Procedures" involves checking, compacting, and logically and physically storing the data. Although certain functions in this section are not universally required at present, there is a trend toward this requirement.

The functional requirements for tying together the various parts of the data management system to the application program are given in the subsection entitled "Data Base Interface." The data base administration functions are discussed separately in section 2-3. Included is the requirement to allow user and data base administrator written code in the form of data base procedures.

2-1. User Functions

Inquiry

Inquiry is a basic function of all data base management systems. It requires selecting one or more records, extracting the specified fields or items within the record, perhaps doing computation on those items, organizing them in some sort of order, and presenting the results to the user. Each of these areas is considered in more detail in the following paragraphs.

Selection. Selection involves identifying one or more records of interest, as shown in figure 2-1. This identification may be based on content or position. If the selection is by content, the user specifies the records by values within the record. For example, "List employees where department equals production."

There are two basic forms of keyword predicates used in content-based

Employee Records

Name	Department	Job Code	Skill Code
Barry, R.	Production	12	83
Dent, J.	Shipping	14	14
French, J.	Engineering	32	32
George, P.	Production	12	81
Smith, D.P.	Production	8	81
Taylor, W.	Shipping	14	14
Mannes, H.H.	Engineering	32	33

Figure 2-1. Selection.

selection. The first of these is "variable," "relational operator," and "value." Possible relational operators include equal, not equal, greater than, less than, greater than or equal, or less than or equal. In the previous example, DEPARTMENT equals 'PRODUCTION' is this type of predicate. The second predicate form is "variable," "relational operator," and "variable." For example, "List employees where job code is not equal to skill code." Variables can be either in the same or different records. Variables in two different record types are used in more complex queries. For example, "List all the employees in each department where the department expenses are greater than the department budget."

These two basic forms of predicates can be combined in very complex Boolean expressions. For example, "List all the engineers in the production department who have been with the company at least 5 years or have a masters degree." These complex expressions are also considered in more detail in a later section.

Records may also be selected by position. For example, given a particular record, select the next record or select the previous record. Most selection in current data base management systems (DMS 1100,[1] DMS 90,[2] TOTAL,[3] IMS,[4] and so on) is performed in this manner. Moving from one record to the next involves pointers either embedded within the record or stored separately in pointer arrays or index tables. When selection is done by position, the user must know the data structure in order to select records. This type of selection requires more skilled and better trained users. It also involves a much longer development time and higher costs for new applications. Typically, FIND, GET, and FETCH commands are all based on position addressing. Even with some of the higher-level languages such as QLP 1100, the DBMS still finds records based on position even though it may appear to the user as content addressing.[5] The high-level query processing software simply converts the user's content-based query into a series of position-based references executed by the DBMS.

With position addressing, a single record at a time is selected. With content-based addressing, there is no theoretical limit to the number of records that can be selected at one time. Since most users require more than one record per transaction or batch execution of their program, it follows that content addressing would offer performance improvement to the typical data management system user.[6] Therefore, content based addressing is a requirement for record selection.

Record selection through its position in relation to another record (NEXT or PRIOR) can also be supported by a content-based implementation. In this case, the positional relationship is encoded as a data item and stored as part of the record. Then selection is made based on this value. This capability is required for those users who use NEXT or PRIOR type commands to obtain some user-defined ordering of the data records.

Projection. Projection, as shown in figure 2-2, retrieves the fields within a record that are actually needed as opposed to selection, which identifies the records of interest.[7] Projection operates on sets of records and is usually used in conjunction with selection. Projection takes the form of a string of variables that specify the fields desired. This operation is useful because in many cases only a small part of each record is actually needed to answer a particular query. As an example, in building a company phone directory, all that is needed from the employee records are name, department, phone number, and mail station, not salary and skill code.

Join. Join is a concatenation of two records of different types selected by the values of a common field.[8] For example, if a report needs both department- and employee-associated information, department records and the employee records are "joined" on the department code, as shown in figure 2-3. The join uses a type two predicate, where the two variables are the same but in different records. The function of the join is to provide a content-based method for relating owner and member record types in sets.

   In the formal definition the join concatenates the two records. Because not all fields may be needed, however, projection can be used to identify the desired fields. As an extreme case, only the common field may be needed from one of the record types. Combining projection with the join may create a problem. When certain fields are eliminated from one record type, there may be duplicate records. Therefore, a data base management system should provide two options, one that returns all the records and one that eliminates the duplicates.

Derivation. A data item defined in a data base may be either stored or derived. A stored item actually exists within the data base. For a derived item, a rule is given for calculating or determining its value. The value for the item is then derived whenever it is requested. For example, the total price on a bill may be defined as the derived item the sum of the individual charges. When a request is made for the total, the individual charges are added up and returned to the user. There is a tradeoff between the space needed to store the item and the processing needed to determine the value whenever the item is requested. Derived items also can improve data base consistency and reduce update complexity. For example, consider a department record with an item called "average salary." If the item is derived, it is calculated each time it is needed, which is probably infrequently. If the item is stored, however, it must be changed whenever personnel are transferred into or out of the department or whenever someone in the department has a salary adjustment.

   There are two types of derived items. First, an item may be derived from other fields within the same record. This is a simple derivation and easy to support. The second derivation involves values for a set of records,

Employee Records

Name	Dept.	Phone	Mail Stn.	Skill Code	Salary
Barry, R.	502	2165	208	83	15000
Dent, J.	571	3777	312	14	11500
French, J.	540	2821	225	32	23275
George, P.	502	2504	215	81	17500
Smith, D.P.	502	2504	215	81	15000
Taylor, W.	571	3664	304	14	11000
Mannes, H.H.	540	2829	204	33	20550

Figure 2-2. Projection.

Employee Records

Name	Dept.	Skill Code	Salary
Barry, R.	502	83	15000
Dent, J.	571	14	11500
French, J.	540	32	23275
George, P.	502	81	17500
Smith, D.P.	502	81	15000
Taylor, W.	571	14	11000
Mannes, H.H.	540	33	20550

Department Records

Dept.	Director	Budget	Location
502	Jones, P.	1,500,000	Roseville
513	Anderson, D.	175,000	Roseville
540	Gold, G.A.	750,000	Roseville
571	Whitney, D.	175,000	Roseville
618	Poppel, B.	2,225,000	Green Lake
650	Hsiao, Y.	57,000	Green Lake

Figure 2-3. Join.

for example, average salary. These derivations are much more complex and time consuming.

Computations. A derivation may require a series of computations. This may require processing a complete set of records or a file to determine the derived value. Functions currently supported in many DBMSs include COUNT, TOTAL, AVERAGE, MAXIMUM, and MINIMUM. In position-oriented DBMSs, however, the user frequently must explicitly obtain each record and do these computations within the application program. Two examples of queries doing these computational functions are (1) "Print the average salary of all employees in the production department," and (2) "List all the engineers whose current salary is more than 120 percent of the average salary for all engineers."

Ordering. Ordering determines the sequence in which records are stored or retrieved and presented to the user. If the ordering is done with respect to storage, it becomes part of the data base definition or schema. Only one data item can be used for storage-based ordering, that is, physical ordering. Therefore, if there are two "primary keys" in the record, the records will not be in the desired order with respect to one of the keys. Ordering is also a problem with a single key if a record is a member of multiple sets. In this case, the records can be ordered only according to their membership in only one set. In many cases, however, different users need to retrieve records in different orders. Therefore, it is more desirable to specify ordering at retrieval time. As with selection, ordering may be done by content or position. Ordering based on content is more user oriented; for example, "List the employees alphabetically." Position ordering can be for either of two purposes. In many cases it is done strictly for efficiency. In other cases, position ordering is used to implement a particular data structure, for example, a stack or a queue. These data structures, however, can be implemented by time stamping the records and ordering them on retrieval according to the time stamp. Therefore, the ordering requirement should be based on content rather than position and should be submitted at retrieval rather than data definition time.

Updating

Updating involves changing the data base or adding or deleting records or items within records. The focus here is on the contents of the data base, not its definition or how it is stored. These areas are considered in the subsection entitled "Data Base Administration."

Addition. Addition involves increasing the size of the data base. This means adding individual items to a record or adding entire new records to the data base. The addition of records may involve either a single record or a set of records. Addition requires the allocation of additional storage. This requires a decision to determine where to place the new record. This placement is much easier if the information is not stored in specific order. If the data are ordered, the record must be inserted in the proper location by either physically moving records or modifying pointers. In a content-based data management system, addition does not require pointer changes.

Deletion. Deletion, the complement of addition, involves removing either items or records from the data base. This may be performed either physically or logically, by indicating that the item or record is no longer part of the data base. In the former case, physical space is actually freed. Only in the case of physical deletion does the ordering of the data have an effect on the operation's time, with the deletion of ordered data requiring more overhead.

Modification. Modification involves changing the value of an item that already exists in the data base. This does not require additional storage allocation. If the records are ordered, changing the key item is more complicated than changing a nonkey item because the record may have to be moved to maintain the ordering. If the records are unordered, the modification is relatively simple, regardless of whether a key or nonkey item is changed.

There are two types of changes to items within the data base, content independent and content dependent. With content-independent changes, the new value does not depend on the old value; for example, "Enter a customer's new address." With content-dependent changes, the new value is a function of an old value. Frequently, it is only a function of the item being changed; for example, "Reduce the inventory count by 10." In general, however, a content-dependent change simply means a new value for an item is determined by certain other values. A procedure is required to prevent multiple users from modifying any of the items on which the new value is based until the operation is completed. In the simple case, such as the inventory example, this is accomplished by locking only the item to be changed. If items in 10 records are used to compute a new value, however, all those records must be locked before the change is actually calculated and made.

Replacement. Replacement is a special case of modification in which every field in the record is changed. For fixed-length records, this stores a new record in the data base in the position which was used by a previous record. In other words, it is an addition without requiring additional physical space. For variable-length records, additional storage is not required unless the replacement record has added fields or increased the size of previously established fields.

Creation. Creation allows the user to define a file or set of records as his or her own private copy. In contrast to selection, the records defined or selected by a create command are actually stored for the user according to his or her subschema. The DBMS does not recognize that these records are copies, and therefore, when the records in the data base are changed, the user's copy is not changed. In other words, the data base does not provide copy management facilities to maintain multiple copies. The importance of this function is in testing and debugging, where parts of the data base frequently are used for test data. Create allows the user to freeze a part of the data base and use it for testing, rather than constantly using different test data.

Destruction. Destruction is simply the inverse of creation. It involves eliminating the user's private copy.

Qualification

Qualification is the means of defining which records are to be selected. Qualification is usually done with *IF* and *WHERE* clauses. This qualification may involve either content or position.

Content. Content-based qualification uses the previously described two types of predicates, with variables being either real or derived. A simple qualification involves only a single predicate. However, the qualification may take the form "predicate," "logical operation," and "predicate." This can be extended to any number of predicates. For example, a complex qualification may involve identifying all the employees who are engineers in the production department, have been with the company for at least 5 years, and have had one or more management positions. This is a relatively simple query to express using a content-based qualification. It becomes much more difficult, however, if the qualification is based on position. In addition, there is no limit to the number of records that may be selected by a content-based qualification.

Position. Many DBMSs currently use position to determine the record to be selected. This usually involves the currency pointer to a single record or to one record in each set. Other records are selected by moving to the next or prior record or up or down a hierarchy. This is usually done for processing efficiency or to implicitly define a data structure such as a stack or a queue. Position-based qualification is far more difficult to use than content-based qualification, partly because it points to a single record at a time, and partly because the user must know the data structure to move through a set of records. Moreover, the user must check each record as it becomes the current record to determine if it qualifies and should be selected.

2-2. System Functions

Control

There are three basic control functions a DBMS must perform. First, the transactions, whether queries or modifications of the data base, must be assigned a priority. Second, certain backup and recovery operations must be performed by the system. Third, security consideration must be built into the system to control access and handle attempted security violations.

Priority. The DBMS must have a flexible method to assign and change the priority of a transaction. For example, short high-priority transactions must be able to interrupt or preempt long lower-priority transactions. These priorities may be assigned statically when the transaction or user is defined to the DBMS. The user, however, also should be able to dynamically assign a specific priority to an individual request when it is entered. This user-defined priority is but one of the many factors considered by the DBMS and operating system scheduling algorithms. The actual scheduling is dynamically adjusted to take advantage of specific conditions whenever they arise. For example, if certain information needed to process a query is already in the system, greater efficiency may be obtained by increasing the priority of the other transaction needing that information, thereby avoiding reloading the same information later. A final way priorities may be handled is to assign a deadline when the transaction must be completed. As this deadline approaches, the transaction receives a higher priority in order to ensure completion by the deadline.

Backup and Recovery. The DBMS must provide backup and recovery procedures for three situations. First, if all or part of the data base is lost, the data base must be reconstructed. Second, if an error enters into the data base, all following transactions effected by the error must be rolled back. There is a difference if the error is discovered immediately, that is, while the transaction is still active, or later after that transaction no longer exists.

Third, if a deadlock is detected between two users, one of the users must be rolled back. To allow for recovery at a later time, a combination of three actions must be taken on an ongoing basis. First, the data base must periodically be dumped. Second, those transactions updating the data base must be logged. Third, before and/or after images of the changes to the data base must be logged.

Logging is done to an audit trail, which the system must automatically maintain. Furthermore, the user should not be able to delete anything from this audit trail. It should be possible for the user, however, to insert additional information into the audit trail.

To ensure that multiple users do not interfere with each other in updating, data items must be locked before they can be updated. These locks may be at the data base, record, or item level. Locks at the file or data base level prevent other users from accessing the data base. At the other extreme, locks at the individual item level may create excess overhead. A compromise frequently used in DBMSs is to lock at the individual record level. KEEP and FREE or HOLD and RELEASE are typical commands used to maintain locks until the data are modified.[9] On the other hand, locking may create a deadlock problem. This occurs when each user has information the other needs but cannot complete the operation and release the data until the other user has released his data.

There are three methods for deadlock control: preorder, presequence, or preempt. With preordering, all the needed records are requested before any of them are locked. With presequencing, the records are requested in a specific sequence. With preemption, any request can be rolled back to resolve the deadlock once it has been detected. When a user obtains a record, any of three situations may arise. First, he may be updating the record, in which case all other updates to that record must be prevented. Second, he may be reading the record and processing it in a way that would be invalid if the record were changed. For example, all journal updates must stop while a trial balance is being generated. Otherwise, there is the risk of including half a transaction and not being able to balance the accounts. Third, the user may be processing the data base in such a way that updates do not pose a problem, for example, generating a statistical report. It is only in this last case that locking is unnecessary.

Security. Security controls are provided to prevent unauthorized users from obtaining information from the data base. This can be done through appropriate access controls, data encryption, or both.

There are three levels of access controls. The simplest level involves controlling the operation. Many users may be allowed to retrieve from the data base, but only a few may be allowed to modify it. The security access control would prevent the user from doing an operation for which he was not authorized. At the second level the user's access rights may be limited to certain data items in the data base. Both these access controls can be resolved by examining the schema before the request is processed. At the third level, content-based security, the DBMS must examine the selected records to determine if the user is authorized to access them. Although this capability is not provided by most DBMSs, it is needed. For example, in a medical information system, a physician should be able to see a patient's entire medical record, but only the records for his patients. Using a MACRO facility, a data base administrator should be able to define additional access-control procedures. As a general rule, any selection expression that can be used in a query should be an acceptable security restriction.

Data encryption provides further security by concealing the meaning of data. Encryption will become much more important in the future because of the federal encryption standards, the increased use of data communications, and increasing concern with privacy. Therefore, a data encryption capability should be available for installation in the DBMS for those users who require this degree of security.

Data Procedures

Schema-Subschema Conversion. The schema provides a complete logical and physical definition of the data base. The subschema provides the logical definition of the data as the user sees them. The DBMS uses these two definitions to convert the data from their stored form to the form the user expects, thereby providing greater data independence than in file systems. There is an obvious tradeoff in the functionality of this conversion. The more conversion capability provided, the more processing required. The less the user must do, however, the easier the system will be to use. The trend is to increase the functional capabilities of this procedure because it will reduce application development and conversion activities, which are highly labor-intensive and therefore expensive.

Integrity. Data base integrity has three components: (1) ensuring data validity, (2) ensuring data base consistency, and (3) the provisions for backup and recovery discussed previously.

Ensuring data validity is one of the important requirements of the integrity function. Anything that the user has specified to the system about the data base should be automatically maintained by the system. The most common types of validation information involve data values and data structure.

A set of values (for example, state abbreviations or department codes) or a range of values (for example, between 1 and 10) may be specified.

When these values are given, the DBMS should check to ensure that for any of the items so defined, a new value meets the validation criteria. There also can be validation information about the data structure. For example, all employees can belong to only one department or no employee can work on more than three projects. In this case, the system would check to ensure that the data structure constraints are also maintained. In the subsection entitled "Inquiry," a distinction was made between stored and derived items. If a derived item becomes a stored item, its derivation rule becomes part of its validation criteria. For example, if the total charge on a bill is stored, then the validation criteria is that it must equal the sum of the individual items.

Concurrency control is also a part of data base integrity. When multiple users are trying to update the same item in a data base, interference is possible. Therefore, there must be access controls to allow only one user to update an item at a time. If there are value–dependent modifications, the entire group of items on which the new group is based must be controlled to ensure that none of the values are changed before the value–dependent modifications are finished. The primary means of maintaining this type concurrency control is again through access–control locks.

Data Compression. A few DBMSs provide a data compression capability. Whereas, with encryption, data values are modified to conceal the meaning, data compression is used to save space. For example, rather than using state names, two–letter abbreviations may be used to reduce the storage required. Alternatively, because there are only fifty states, each state can be assigned a number which reduces the state code to only six bits. These are examples of compressing a variable–length field to a shorter fixed–length field. In general, there are four cases: the data value being compressed can be either fixed or variable in length and the code into which it is compressed can be fixed or variable in length. The tradeoff with data compression is additional processing time to encode and decode the values versus the storage required for the uncompressed values. Storage savings of over 50 percent are frequent when appropriate data compression methods are used.

The key for determining the appropriate coding method depends on the probability of value occurrences. If there is a field where all the values are equally likely, compression is only beneficial in reducing a longer value to a shorter code, for example, encoding state names. In cases where certain values occur far more frequently than others, additional benefits can be obtained by storing the most frequent values using very short codes and less frequent values using longer codes. Huffman encoding is an example of this method.[10] Ideally, the user should have the option to specify whether or not a data item is compressed. This option is important because if an item is already compressed, trying to compress it again would lengthen rather than shorten the field. Also the user should be able to choose specific data compression algorithms, selecting the most effective one for his application. This requires providing entry points where the user can integrate his own routine into the DBMS.

Data Base Interface

This subsection describes the type of interfaces required between the DBMS and the user or data base administrator. There is a permanent link between the data base and the schema which describes it and between the various user subschemas and the schema to which they apply. Given these permanent linkages, other interfaces must be provided between the user and the DBMS and between the user and that part of the data base which will be used.

Data Management System Interface. This provides the linkage between the individual user, the subschema which describes the data base as he sees it, and the data base itself. The linkages between the subschema and the schema and between the schema and data base are already established and do not need to be established for each run unit.

File Linkage. This linkage connects the run unit to that part of the data base which it uses. The primary function is to open and close a specific part of the data base, for example, a physical area. In addition, when a user opens an area or part of the data base, he should also specify how he will be using that area—read only, update, or exclusive use. Usage of the data base is subject to acccess constraints provided by the security and integrity definition implementations. For example, if security restricts a user only to reading the data base and not to updating it, then he would be prevented from opening the data base for update.

2–3. Administration Functions

Data Base Administration

In a data base environment, certain functions must be performed by a central authority—the data base administrator. The data base administrator (DBA) must define the data base after considering the requirements of all the users and making the necessary performance tradeoffs. He also must generate or populate the data base once it has been defined. Finally, as the data base is used and requirements change, the DBA must be able to redefine or reorganize the data base to meet evolving user needs.

Definition. The data base administrator must define the data base. This definition includes the logical data structure, the validation criteria, the physical structure, the location, and the format of the data. The data base describes or models the real world with which the user must deal. The data base administrator must make sure that the logical definition he uses is compatible with this real-world model. To accomplish this, he defines different record types, relationships among them, and the data items for each type. Part of the definition of the data items include integrity constraints and the types of values these items can maintain. For example, a data item may be numeric, but it may be stored as either integer, floating point, or double precision. Other items may be text in ASCII, FIELD-DATA, or BCD.

The data base administrator also must have the ability to define new data types as they are needed. This means defining the set of values or range of values that is valid for a particular type of item. Moreover, validation procedures or the checks to be made to ensure the integrity of the data item must be defined. All the logical, structural, and validation constraints which the data base administrator defines to the DBMS should be automatically maintained.

In addition to entering the data base with various access methods, different users also view the data with different logical structures. One user may view a network, another a hierarchy, and a third user a set of relations. The data base administrator must make the appropriate tradeoffs between these structures and store the data base itself in the appropriate structure so that all users can get at the data base using the view they consider appropriate. This requires a common underlying data model with the ability to translate between various logical structures. To do this, the data base administrator must define the schema and work with the users to define their subschemas and to ensure that the appropriate schema-to-subschema mapping is possible for all user subschemas.

Different users need to access the data base in different ways. The data base administrator, therefore, must make the proper tradeoffs and determine the most effective access methods, for example, direct addressing, hashing, indexed sequential, or via record sets in current systems.

Data Base Generation. Once the DBA has defined the data base, it must be created or populated with the users' data. This generation should be performed with a DBMS routine. This can be done if the system provides a way for the DBA to describe the current data format and the schema with which the data should conform. As the data base is loaded, the DBMS routines check for conformance to the schema. The important point is that these checks are made as part of the DBMS procedures as the data base is loaded into the system. Therefore, invalid data can be detected and corrected before they are entered in the data base.

Redefinition. After the data base has been used for some time, user requirements usually change. New information must be added to the data base and additional constraints are imposed or company policies may change, all resulting in changes to other constraints within the data base. The DBMS must provide the DBA with the capability to redefine the data base. First, this means changing the schema. Once this is done, the DBMS procedure must look at the new schema and the old schema and assure itself that an appropriate mapping can be carried out. Then the data base or parts of it should be taken off-line and converted from the old definition to its new definition. The important point, under redefinition, is that the schema changes. Therefore, the data base must be changed to conform to the new schema. If it is not possible to map between the new schema and all the sub-schemas, then some of the subschemas must be changed. This is the point at which data independence fails, and some of the applications require changes.

Reorganization. Reorganization occurs when, after extended use, the data base is no longer organized efficiently. The logical definition of the data base, however, does not need to be changed; that is, the schema is not changed. Reorganization involves physically changing the data base to obtain more efficient performance, not changing its structure as the user sees it. For example, records can be deleted logically by setting a delete flag. This creates gaps within the data base which can then be used. Reorganization will then physically delete the records and pack the data base so that processing will be more efficient. In addition, independent parts of the data base should be reorganized independently so that the entire data base is not "down" or unavailable during the reorganization process. The important difference between redefinition and reorganization is that in reorganization the schema itself does not change.

Macro Capability. This allows the data base administrator or the user to define specific procedures as extensions of the DBMS. For example, the data base administrator may specify a particular hashing routine to be used with a certain variable. This macro capability involves two steps: defining the macro, and invoking the macro. This requires defining points within the DBMS at which the user or data base administrator can insert his own code to function as an integral part of the data base management system.

There are two types of macros to be considered. First, there are those written by the data base administrator which become integral parts of the DBMS and which the user never sees. For example, hashing procedures or validation procedures for special data types defined by the installation data base administrator. The second type of macro is defined and invoked by the user. For example, report definition and transaction processing can be defined as macros to be invoked whenever necessary. The important point is that the user-defined macros are still subject to all the constraints and controls of the data base management system. The capability of the macro-definition facility, however, should be such that anything discussed previously under inquiry, updating, or qualification should be allowed. In other words, a user should be able to design a macro using the full range of DBMS capability, subject only to integrity and security constraints previously defined by the data base administrator.

Summary

In this chapter, a set of functional requirements for a data base management system was developed and described. The functions that are actually implemented in the data base computer depend on a number of factors, such as cost/performance and user environment.

Three types of functional requirements—user, system, and data base administration—were identified and discussed. These functions also can be considered in terms of their current availability and use. First, there are the basic requirements, available in most current data base management systems already in widespread use. Next, there are the expanded requirements, common functions that are currently not a part of the DBMS and which users must include in their application programs. Finally, there are the future requirements. These are for those functions currently not being used, but which will be in the future because of either cost/performance improvements of to legislative mandate.

Basic requirements include the capability to select a record or a specified part of a record (projection), to update a record, and to add and delete fields or records. The basic qualification requirement locates data by position. Some of the high-level query languages appear to support content- or value-based qualification. This type of query is not processed directly, but rather translated into a series of position-based queries. In some cases, the translation is not possible and the query cannot be answered.

Basic control functions such as priority definition, backup and recovery, and deadlock prevention or resolution also are available in most current systems and remain requirements. Data base definition, generation, redefinition, and reorganization are also basic requirements. Few systems, however, provide them to the extent needed. Data translation is currently offered at a very low level—data item definition is limited to the current COBOL capability and the subschema can only be a subset of the schema.

The major extensions needed to augment current capabilities are in allowing the user greater flexibility in selecting records based on content and in defining the data. The user must be able to select one or more records with a content-based qualification involving complex Boolean expressions and any data items within the data base. Users today, particularly programming users, frequently do this as part of their application because they are limited to selecting single records from a set based on position. To implement a content-based owner-member set relationship, the relational "join" operator must be supported. Moreover, the user must be able to order the selected records on any data item.

For improved data integrity, significant extensions are needed in the data definition capability. It should be possible to define valid ranges or sets of values for an item or to specify more complex validation rules. It should be possible to define a derived item by specifying the derivation rule. Currently only a few standard derivations—COUNT, TOTAL, AVERAGE, MAXIMUM, and MINIMUM—are available. Finally, security access control must be extended to allow content-based security restrictions instead of just data item or schema level restrictions.

Future requirements include data encryption and more advanced data compression. Encryption will become much more important in the future because of federal encryption standards and increased concern with privacy.

Notes

1. Sperry Univac, *Data Management System* [*DMS 1100*], UP7907 Rev. 3, 1977.

2. Sperry Univac, *Data Management System* [*DMS 90*], UP-8366 Rev. 1, 1978.

3. Varian Data Machines, *V70 Total Data Base Management System Reference,* 1975.

4. IBM, *IMS/VS Programmer Reference and Operator's Manual,* SH20-9047-0, April 1975.

5. Sperry Univac, *Query Language Processor* [*QLP 1100*], UP-8231 Rev. 1, 1977.

6. O.H. Bray and H.A. Freeman, "Data Usage and the Data Base Processor," *Proceedings of the ACM '78,* December 1978, pp. 234-240.

7. E.F. Codd, "A Relational Model of Data for Large Shared Data Banks," *Communications of the ACM* 13, No. 6, June 1970, pp. 377-387.

8. Ibid.

9. Sperry Univac, *Query Language Processor;* Sperry Univac, *Data Management System* [*DMS 1100*].

10. S.R. Ruth and P.J. Kreutzer, "Data Compression for Large Business Files," *Datamation,* September 1972, pp. 62-66.

3

An Example Data Base

This chapter describes an example data base, different methods of organizing and accessing the data, and a typical set of transactions against the data base to elucidate the operation of a data base computer and to compare the various DBC designs. In this chapter, the transactions are processed against three forms of the same data base installed on a general-purpose computer. In chapter 5, these same transactions are described for each type of data base computer architecture. The data base chosen is a subset of a much larger one that is typical of manufacturing management and operational control systems. The first section presents a view of the overall manufacturing application, a data base design for it, and a description of the particular subset selected. This includes both the requirements of the application and the logical structure of the data base.

The next two sections examine this data base and the transactions against it in terms of a network or CODASYL and a relational implementation. In each section, the basic concepts underlying that type of DBMS are presented, the logical and physical structure of the data base is considered, and the way that the selected transactions are processed against the data base are described.

For both the CODASYL and relational systems, the information the users require and the changes they enter are equivalent. With this being the case, an examination of the DBMSs yields more similarities than differences in the two types. Both systems identify and describe entities using record types and relations, respectively. Both have ways of linking different types of entities into sets, either statically when the data base is designed (CODASYL) or dynamically when a transaction is presented (relational). The most significant difference usually considered is the level of the query language. The assumption is that CODASYL systems use low-level, record-at-a-time languages but that relational systems have high-level, set-oriented ones. Although this may have been true at one time, many CODASYL DBMSs now include a high-level query language on top of the conventional low-level data manipulation language, while some relational systems are physically implemented using CODASYL-type networks. These similarities will become more apparent with the transaction processing and conversion discussions in this chapter.

The last section of this chapter discusses many of the factors involved in converting from a CODASYL to a relational system. Since many current DBMS installations are CODASYL-based, while most of the special-purpose data base computer designs support relational-based data bases more effectively, this conversion is an important prerequisite for widespread data base computer system use.

3-1. Manufacturing Application and Data Base

Overview

A manufacturing firm purchases raw materials and converts them into the finished goods or products it sells. The actual production processes vary greatly depending on the product and the production methods used. Most companies that use mass production methods will differ significantly from smaller job shops or special-order producers. In the marketing and inventory control area, though, there are many similarities. Therefore, the example data base described in this chapter will concentrate on this area.

The customers of all these types of manufacturers are either the final end users of the product or middlemen, wholesalers, or retailers. As far as the manufacturer is concerned, however, there is little difference among them other than the quantities they buy.

Most manufacturing firms have several distinct product lines. Each of these lines is made up of a variety of models of different sizes, colors, features, and prices. One or more production lines may be used for each product, with each production line consisting of a number of work stations with different machine tools and personnel with different skills. In some cases, a production line may be designed for and restricted to producing only a single product. In other cases, especially with the smaller companies, the production line must be flexible and able to produce several different products. The manufacturing schedule determines how many of which products to produce and schedules the production on the various machines. Changing a machine from one product to another requires a certain setup time, which is then amortized over the total production run.

Various raw materials are used in the manufacturing process. In some cases these materials are processed and modified, while in other cases they are simply assembled into a finished product. Regardless of how they are used, certain quantities are maintained in inventory. Materials are taken from the inventory for production and added to inventory as received from the various suppliers.

In summary, the manufacturing process involves tracking and monitoring many types of entities. A partial list includes raw materials, purchase orders, line items within a purchase order, suppliers, departments, machine tools and work stations, labor, products, customers, customer orders, line items within customer orders, and work in progress. The data base for a complex manufacturing system must support both day-to-day operations and periodic management reporting requirements. The data base management system must be able to generate a number of standard management reports as well as answer a variety of both simple and complex ad hoc queries and data base modification requests.

The officers, directors, and other management personnel require an enormous amount of information to make the proper decisions. Much of this information can or should be obtained from the wealth of data that was gathered and stored in the data base. Through the DBMS, these people should be able to ask such questions as: Which of our customers provide our grestest dollar volume in sales? Which are our most profitable customers? Which products have the greatest sales volume and the greatest profit? Given our current inventory of machine tools and equipment, what is our most profitable product mix? Given our current production schedules and supplier prices, which components or subassemblies of our products should we make and which should we buy? What inventory policies are best to minimize our total inventory costs?

In terms of the day-to-day operations of the company, many other types of DBMS transactions are required. Many of these are relatively simple and frequently require only the retrieval or update of a single record. Examples of these types are accepting and entering customer orders; generating necessary supporting documentation such as packing slips, bills of lading, and invoices; and keeping track of back orders to ensure that they are filled when the back-ordered parts are received. In addition, operations personnel answering customer inquiries about the status of various orders, shipments, and invoices results in another set of transactions.

To ensure smooth operations, the inventory must be effectively used and managed. This requires constantly knowing the quantity, location, and value of all the various items in the finished goods, raw materials, and work-in-process inventories. Moreover, the data base must track the many documents relating to additions to and depletion of each of these inventories. For example, purchase orders to suppliers indicate future increases to the raw materials inventory, while production schedules indicate future reductions of this inventory. By monitoring the actual and projected depletion of the raw materials inventory, those items whose reorder point has been reached can be identified. Purchase orders can be prepared and sent to the appropriate suppliers. Bills of lading and invoices can be reconciled and the appropriate payments made.

Within the actual production area, schedules can be planned that include tools to be used, setup times, production times, and maintenance times. In the job-shop environment, actual orders can be tracked through all the work stations for improved productivity and faster response to customer orders.

All this manufacturing activity requires a very complex data base for support. The example data base used in this chapter, however, does not contain this level of complexity. For clarity and ease of explanation, it focuses only on a subset of the complete data base and includes only parts, products, customers, customer orders, and line items within the customer orders. There is also a symmetry between the purchase of parts and the sale of products. This initial overview of the manufacturing operation and the complete data base is provided to indicate that the example data base and the transactions on which the later analyses are based is a typical subset of a common data base and its applications.

Transactions

This subsection identifies a set of typical transactions, representing a variety of types of data base processing requirements which will be applied to the example data base. Some transactions involve locating a single record, given its key. Some involve locating a single record, but require examining certain fields within the record to determine if it is the desired one. Other transactions require scanning an entire set of records which may or may not be clustered. Still other transactions involve modifying records or inserting or deleting records. Finally, there are some complex queries which require processing all the records in a set and reordering them before presentation to the user. All the transactions used in this chapter are presented in terms of high-level queries in order to be more meaningful to the reader. However, when they are processed by the DBMS, especially by a CODASYL DBMS, they frequently must be decomposed into a series of more basic, low-level operations.

The simplest transactions require only listing certain fields within records specified by their keys. For example:

List the ship-to-address for customer *ABC*.

List the inventory level for part *xyz*.

Slightly more complex queries require listing all the members of an easily defined set.

List all the order numbers for customer *ABC*.

List all the items in customer order 1234.

Slightly more complex queries do not explicitly identify the set to be processed. Some initial searching must be performed to locate the set. An example is

List all the items in customer *ABC*'s latest order.

Other transactions require updating the data base. Some transactions simply change a field in a record already in the data base, while others add or delete entire records from the data base. Included in this category are

Reduce the inventory level of part *xyz* by 100.

Add new customer *DEF* to the data base.

Add a new order (number 4567) for customer *ABC*.

Add an item to order 1234.

Delete part *xyz* from the inventory.

Other types of transactions involve deriving such information as totals, counts, or averages from sets of records. Other transactions identify a set of records and perform the same operation on every record in the set. Examples of these types are

How many customer orders are there?

Calculate the total value of all customer orders.

What is the average value of customer orders?

Calculate the total value of the inventory.

Add 10 percent to the price of item *xyz* for all orders after June 1, 1979.

Finally, there are very complex transactions which frequently result in many separate data base queries. While they represent a single transaction from the user's point of view, separate application programs are needed because current high-level query languages cannot yet handle them. An example of this type of very complex query is

Generate monthly bills for all customers.

Since this can be thought of in terms of combinations of those previously listed types of transactions, it will not be specifically treated to avoid being repetitive.

3-2. The CODASYL Data Base

A CODASYL or network-structured data base consists of a collection of one or more record types corresponding to types of real-world entities such as customers, orders, and parts. Each entity type has characteristics or attributes that are described by the various fields within the record. For example, a customer may have an identification number, an address, a credit rating, an outstanding balance, and a number of orders in progress. Certain attributes, such as identification number, uniquely identify specific entities, while others, such as balance and credit rating, are simply descriptive.

Part of the data base definition consists of a complete description of each record type. Although most of what is known about the data is provided to the DBMS in the schema using a data description language (DDL), some characteristics cannot be expressed. These characteristics, therefore, are known only external to the DBMS and cannot be automatically checked and maintained for the user. The record description consists of two parts:

1. A complete description of each field within the record.
2. Location and placement of the record within the data base.

The field description includes the item name, length, and how it is to be used. The definition also specifies whether or not the item can be repeated within the record and, if so, the number of times it may occur or on what the number of occurrences depends. Additional information is provided on whether the item functions as a key, with or without duplicates, or simply as a descriptor. All this information can be used by the DBMS to ensure the validity of the data as they are entered in the data base. Although most DBMSs allow only this relatively limited data item description, the data base administrator (DBA) may know much more about the item. Included in the DBA's knowledge may be the acceptable set of values or the range of values the item can assume, the type of data item and therefore the legitimate operations on the item, and whether the item is mandatory or optional in the record.

Part of the record description also defines where the record is placed in the data base and how it is located. The three placement and retrieval methods are

1. DIRECT
2. CALC or hashed
3. VIA a set of which the record is a member

Using the direct method, the user specifies the relative physical storage location of the record. This approach is undesirable because it binds the application too closely to the actual physical layout of the data base and to physical storage devices.

CALC is the usual method employed to retrieve a specific record within the data base. By specifying the values of the key fields within the record, which is then translated or "hashed" to obtain the record storage location, the user can obtain a single record. This approach requires, in most cases, only a single reference to the data base. However, the DBMS will automatically follow any overflow chains if necessary to retrieve the record. The CALC key itself may be composed of several fields within the record and does not necessarily have to be unique. Any field or set of fields within the record can be used as the CALC key, but it must be specified when the data base is created because it determines where the data are stored.

Finally, records may be located using VIA. This location method is dependent on the concept of a set, discussed in the following paragraphs.

The concept of a set is essential to all types of data bases, although it is most obvious with the network structures. All the data base definitions previously described refer to records of a single type. Since almost all data bases involve records or entities of many types, the concept of a set provides a means of relating these different types. For example, customer records must be related to order records, which in turn must be related to the appropriate product or item records. This is accomplished by establishing owner and member records for each set. Although only one type of record can be an owner for a set, there can be several different types of member records in that set. In addition, a record type can be in any number of sets. For example, a part record can be a member of sets relating it to a supplier, a customer order, and the products in which the part is used. A single record occurrence, however, can be a member of only one occurrence of the same set. This restriction is impractical for many applications. For example, the same part may be ordered by several customers. This problem is resolved by using an intermediate record type, that is, item, which only has to be linked to a single occurrence of each set.

A record type may be a member of either "manual" or "automatic" sets. For an automatic set, the DBMS automatically links the members of the set and maintains their order. For a manual set, the application program itself must do this linking and order maintenance. Membership in automatic sets is mandatory with every instance of the member record type linked to an owner record thus creating a set occurrence. With manual sets, some memberships are optional, and a member record can exist without being linked to an owner. For example, a new part in inventory not yet ordered by any customer cannot be linked to any order record. When the necessary conditions for set membership are met, the member record can then be linked or attached to the proper owner record for the specific set occurrence.

There are many possible placements of a new record into a set. It may be inserted first in the set, last in the set, or in a particular place according to a specified key value. Also, a new member record can be inserted either before or after the record currently selected by the user. If the set definition allows member records with duplicate keys, the DBMS must be told whether to insert them, before or after the existing record with the same key value.

Sets may be physically implemented in several ways. In one case, a record is linked with pointers to the next member of each set of which it is a member. Each member record in the set also may be linked to the owner of the set or only the last member of the set may be linked to the owner. To retrieve an entire set, then, each member record in the set must be retrieved and examined in order to find the pointer to the next member of the set. If all the members of the set are clustered such that retrieval occurs in a single mass storage access, performance is not a serious problem. In many cases, however, this clustering is not possible, and the performance can be quite poor, with many accesses required to obtain the entire set. An alternative implementation of this case is through the use of a pointer array or index table, where all the pointers are extracted from the records and are maintained in a separate table. This method requires one mass storage access for the pointer and at least one other access for the data records. With pointer arrays, the order of record retrieval can be planned, usually providing better performance.

In either of the two variations of a pointer-based system, critical information, that is, set membership, is provided by the pointers. Transactions that specify nonkey fields for selection, however, cannot be easily processed because pointers were not previously established for these fields. Thus the user is required to examine all the records of a particular type or in a particular set and to evaluate the selection expression for each record as part of the application program.

A second method of set implementation is to embed in both the owner and the member records the key fields that determine set membership. For example, given a customer-order set, the order record would include the customer number. This allows owner records (customers) to be identified by examining the member records (customer orders). It is more difficult, however, to use this method to find all the members of a set given its owner, because, as in this example, the maximum number of orders a customer could have is usually indeterminable. Therefore, there is no limit to the number of record occurrences. It is possible to combine this embedded key method with the pointer approach in a CODASYL data base. For example, each order record may contain the customer number to facilitate processing as well as pointers linking the order records to the customer records to obtain faster access.

The structure of the example CODASYL data base is shown in figure 3-1, and the record types are contained in table 3-1. The data base contains five record types and five sets. One record type was established for a customer and one for an order and a set established to link each customer to his

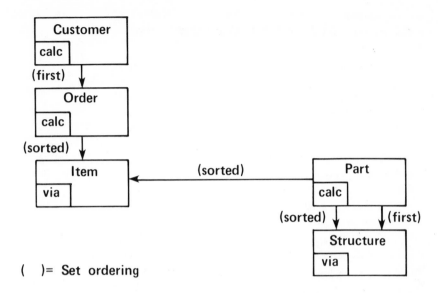

Figure 3-1. CODASYL Data Base Structure.

orders. Any customer or order record can be retrieved by specifying its key, the customer or order number. Corresponding to each order, there can be any number of items, thereby constituting a third record type. A second set type links the item records to the appropriate order, with the item records located through (VIA) the appropriate order. Each member record of this set has an embedded pointer to one or more other records in the set as well as a pointer to the owner record. New order records are added at the beginning of the customer–order chain to avoid processing the entire chain, since application activities typically concentrate on the most recent orders. New items within an order, however, are inserted in a sorted sequence based on an item–sequence number key.

There are two additional record types and three sets that relate to the parts in the inventory. First, there are randomly accessible part records and a set relating parts to items within an order. As was the case with the set linking items to orders, item records in this set can be located only through the appropriate owner record (a parts record). Second, there is also a record for each structure, either assembly or subassembly, which is related to parts records through two sets. For both these, parts is the owner–record type and the structure records are the members. One set links a part to all the structures in which it is used, and the other links all the structures to the parts which are used in it.

Table 3-1
CODASYL Data Base Record Types

Customer	*Order*
Customer number	Order number
Customer name	Customer number
Address	Ship to address
Credit rating	Date of order
Order numbers	Date closed
	Value
Item	
Item number	*Part*
Order number	Part number
Customer number	Part description
Date created	Date last transaction
Date changed	Date stock taken
Date closed	Inventory at stock
Date required	Inventory current
Date shipped	Discount code
Part number	Reorder point
Quantity	Supplier
Price unit	Supplier number
Price extended	Supplier name
	Cost
	Price
	Delay
Structure	
Part number	
Quantity	

The remainder of this section describes how a CODASYL system, using its low-level data manipulation language, processes some of the typical transactions described previously. It should be emphasized that with a low-level language, such operations as traversing a set and getting the next or prior record of a particular type are performed as part of the application program and not by the DBMS. The DBMS returns only a single record to the application program, which must examine it and then specify the next record desired. The major exception to this procedure is when the DBMS traverses a sorted automatic set to find the proper insertion point for a new record. Obviously, high-level languages built on top of CODASYL DBMSs offer users much greater functional capabilities.

In the following transaction descriptions, the number of accesses specified includes only those required to retrieve or modify the data. If pointer arrays are used, one or more additional accesses are needed to retrieve the pointers. This is especially true for inserts, deletes, or modifications of the key on which the pointer is maintained. Also data validity checking and schema–subschema conversion require parts of both the schema and the subschema and therefore require at least two additional accesses.

List the address for customer *ABC*.

For those record types, such as customer, located by CALC, it is relatively easy to find a desired record, given its key value. In this case, the DBMS converts or hashes the value of the key field into the record's physical storage address and usually retrieves it in a single data base access. With the DBMS automatically processing synonyms and overflow chains, however, the number of accesses averages slightly more than one. Next, the requested fields are extracted from the record, converted to correspond to the subschema definition if necessary, and finally presented to the user.

List all the order numbers for customer *ABC*

This query requires traversing the readily determined set of orders for a specific customer as defined by his key value. As with the previous query, the DBMS first hashes on the customer identifier to locate the specific customer record. The set of all the orders for that customer must then be traversed to obtain the order number from each record. This is accomplished by first obtaining the pointer in the customer record to the order record that is the first member of the set. Then, when the application program requests the first member of the set, that is, the first order for that customer, this record is retrieved and the order number saved. The order record also contains a pointer to the next order in the set, which the user can obtain by issuing a GET NEXT command. This process of issuing GET NEXT requests is repeated until all the orders in the set have been retrieved and the complete set has been traversed.

The number of data base accesses required by this transaction depends on the number of members in the set. Normally, there is one access for the customer record and one access for each of the order records in the set. The number of accesses would be reduced if the orders for a customer were clustered so that several order records could be retrieved with each access. Since both customer and order records are located using CALC, this clustering is unlikely unless the CALC key for the order records includes the customer number as well as the order number.

List all the items in order 1234.

This query is processed similarly to the last one, with one possible variation. In this case, the DBMS first hashes to the record for order 1234. As the user issues a series of GET NEXT requests, the DBMS follows the chain of pointers. One item record at a time is retrieved until all the item records (member records of the set linking an order to all the items within it) are obtained. Since the member records are not located independently but only through a set, when the data base is designed, the set can be clustered by locating the item records near the corresponding order records. This clustering allows a single retrieval to obtain several item records, thereby offering better data base system performance for this type of query than for the previous one. In fact, if the set is small enough, a single access may be all that is needed to obtain the owner and all the members of the set. (Note: A complicating factor is that the item records in the example data base are members of two sets and can be located VIA either set but can be placed near only one owner record type. Therefore, the item records should be clustered near either order or part records depending on which set is referred to more frequently.)

List all the items in customer *ABC*'s latest order.

This query involves three record types and two sets and is processed by the following series of steps. First, the user requests the record for customer *ABC,* which the DBMS obtains through the hashing technique. Then the application program retrieves, through a series of GET NEXT requests, the set of all orders for that customer and records the date of each order. By retrieving all the orders and their dates, the latest order can be identified and the item records for items in that order can be traversed with a series of GET NEXT requests. In the worst case, this transaction requires one access for the customer record, one access for each order record for that customer, and one access for each item within the latest order. Clustering item records is one way to reduce the total number of accesses. Another is to sequence the order records by date, so that the latest order is the first one in the set.

Reduce the inventory level of part *xyz* by 100.

For this transaction type, the DBMS hashes part code *xyz* to locate the part record and then retrieves the record. The data are then locked to prevent another user from concurrently trying to modify them. This allows the inventory level field to be modified and the modified record to be stored back in its original location. Finally, the data are unlocked to enable other users to access them.

Several special cases may exist for this type of transaction. In one, a check could be made to ensure that the inventory level is greater than or equal to 100. If it is not, the transaction is rejected because a negative inventory level has no meaning. This type of check, however, must frequently be made by the application program because this constraint may not be allowed by the data definition. In some cases, the modification may result in expanding the size of the record. When this happens, the record is not stored in its original position but is placed in an overflow area and the original record is deleted. Subsequent attempts by the DBMS to find this part record results in first retrieving a pointer to an overflow area and then retrieving the record with an additional access.

Add new customer *DEF* to the data base.

For this type of transaction, the DBMS translates or hashes the customer identifier to determine where the new record should be stored. Since no duplicates are allowed, it must then check to ensure that no other customer records have that same identifier. If there is another customer with that same identifier, the transaction is rejected. If there is not, space is allocated for the new record, either in the hashed position or in an overflow area, and the record is stored. Prior to actually storing the record, the various fields within the record are checked to ensure that they conform to the validity criteria specified in the schema. If there is a conflict, then, depending on the implementation, either a special code is stored in the invalid field or the entire transaction is rejected. In either case, the user is notified of the error and action is taken.

Add a new order (number 4567) for customer *ABC*.

The first few steps for inserting this record in the data base is the same as for the previous one. The DBMS hashes on the order identifier (4567) to determine where to place the new record. Checks are made to ensure that there are not any other records with the same order number and that all the fields in the record are valid. The record is then stored either in the location specified by its hashed key or in an overflow area. As is the case for the previous example, inserting the new record requires only one access unless an overflow area is needed.

It is at this point that the processing of this transaction type differs from that of the previous one. Order records are specified as members of an automatic set linking them to the appropriate customer records. The DBMS must therefore link this new order to the appropriate set. Using the customer number in the order record, the DBMS first locates the customer record using the hashing technique. The field in the customer record pointing to the first order record is then changed to point to the new order. The pointer field in the new order is subsequently set to point to the next order in the set (the previous first order record pointed to by the customer record). None of the other order records needs to be modified unless both forward and backward pointers were used. If this was the case, then the previous first member of the set would also have to be modified so its prior pointer would now point to the new order record.

To summarize, the insertion of a new record requires one access unless the storage area is full, in which case several accesses are needed. A minimum of one additional access is also required to link the record to each set of which it is a member. Linkage with only one access is possible only if the set is ordered "first"; that is, the owner record points to the last member record inserted. If the set is ordered "last" and does not have backward pointers, then all the members of the set must be retrieved, perhaps with a separate access for each one, in order to find the end of the chain so that the new record can be inserted. If the set is maintained in sorted order, then, on the average, half the members will have to be retrieved to determine where to insert the new record. Finally, for all the set orderings, an additional access is needed if the set is also linked "prior" (backward pointer) as well as "next" (forward pointer).

The DBMS performs all the positioning and linking required to insert a record in all the automatic sets of which it is a member. If the record is a member of a manual set, however, the application program must explicitly locate the insertion point and then issue an ATTACH command to create the links. At this point, the DBMS sets only the pointers in the neighboring records for the specified manual set. This same process must then be repeated for each manual set of which the record is a member.

Add an additional item to order 1234.

This type of insertion is similar to the previous one, with the major difference being the clustering of the item records to improve performance. After the record for order 1234 is located, the set of items for the order is traversed until the proper spot is found for the new record according to its sequence number. The record is then inserted and the necessary pointers changed. The same operation must be performed to link the new item record to the proper parts record, with the number of accesses required depending on where the record is inserted in each of the sets. Since both sets are automatic, however, the DBMS performs all this positioning for the user who had only to issue the simple ADD command.

Delete part *xyz* from the inventory.

Usually, this type of transaction results in logically deleting the record instead of physically deleting the record and shifting another record into that space; that is, the record is simply marked as deleted and the space is freed so it can be reused. Processing this transaction requires, then, that the record be located and modified to indicate it is deleted and a corresponding modification made in a free space table. This operation probably requires at least four accesses, a retrieve and a store for both the modified record (a delete flag has been set) and the free space table.

The deletion process is more complicated if the record is a member of any sets. For sets linked prior and next, a relatively easy modification to the pointers to the appropriate pairs of records can be made which requires only two additional accesses per set. If each record is linked only to the next member of the set, however, the delete is more difficult. The "next" pointer in the deleted record specifies one of its neighbors, which must be retrieved through one access. To locate the prior record for linkage to this one, however, requires traversing the set from the first record to the deleted one, with the number of accesses required depending on the number of records in the set preceding the deleted record. Obviously, if the record is a member of many sets, this deletion process can be very time consuming on conventional computers.

The deletion of the owner of a set is even more complex than deleting a member record. In fact, there are two possible situations. In one case, such as in a hierarchy, the deletion of an owner record requires the deletion of all the member records in the set. In the second case, all the members of the set are not deleted, but they are modified to indicate that they are no longer a part of the set. This may require one access for every member of every set owned by the deleted record.

How many orders are there?

To respond to this type of query, the DBMS retrieves the first order record and returns it to the user. The user must then issue a series of commands, each one requesting the next record of the specified type, that is, an order record. The user himself must keep a count of the number of records retrieved before the end–of–file message is returned. In this case, the user, through the DBMS, is simply traversing a record type similar to the way he traversed a set. Thus the DBMS just retrieves the records for the user to process.

If this last request were implemented as part of a high–level language built on top of a CODASYL system, it could be handled in either of two ways. First, it could be processed as described previously, with the exception that the DBMS would count the orders and send only a final count to the user. The second approach involves the DBMS using certain internal system information not normally available to the user. For example, some DBMSs retain a count of the number of records of each type found in the data base. If this were the case, then this information could be used to answer the query. The more general form of this query type (for example, "How many orders are there for this month?") requires, however, that the DBMS retrieve and examine all the records of a particular type.

Calculate the total value of all orders.

As with the previous transaction, the DBMS retrieves the first record of the type, the user issues a series of GET NEXT commands, and all the records of the specified type are thereby traversed. Instead of simply counting the records, the user saves the value of each order record to construct the total. If a high-level query language were used to express this query type, the DBMS would build up the total for the user and return only the final total. The example data base illustrates the worst case of requiring an access for every order record because the order records are not clustered.

If the data base design does not include the total value of the order in each order record, then an additional step would be required. All the order records would still have to be traversed, but in this case, once one was retrieved, the set of item records for that order would be traversed to compute the total value for each order.

What is the average order value?

This query is simply a combination of the two previous ones. As the order records are traversed, a count of the number of orders and the total value of all the orders are maintained. After all the order records have been processed, the average is computed by either the user, if a low-level language is used, or the DBMS, if a high-level language is used. As with the previous query, the worst case requires one access for each order record.

Add 10 percent to the price of part *xyz* for all orders after June 1, 1979.

This transaction changes the price of the part in every order made after the effective date. The set linking all the item records for that part must be transversed. For each record in that set, the date must be compared to the effective date of the new price. If the date is later, then the price must be checked and changed if it is not equal to the new price. This complex transaction requires one access for the part record and probably one access for each item record. Because the item records are clustered with their corresponding order records and not with the part records, there is little chance that more than one of the required item records will be obtained in a single access.

If the order record contains the total value of the order, then an additional step is required by the transaction. The effect of the change in price (price difference times the quantity) must be calculated and reflected in the order record which is the owner of that item record. This requires that the DBMS locate and modify the owner record. This is not difficult if the order number is also contained in the item record or if the item record is linked to its order record.

This concludes the description of the CODASYL data model and the typical transactions against an example CODASYL data base. These same transactions will be treated next with respect to a relational data base and later, in chapter 5, with respect to the various data base computer architectures.

3-3. The Relational Data Base

The relational data base approach presented in this section offers an alternative to the CODASYL approach. The relational data base describes the same real-world entities and attributes as the CODASYL data base, but with different definitions for parts of the data base and different operations on the data base. This section describes the concepts and data definition for a relational data base for the example manufacturing system. Figure 3-2 illustrates the example relational data base structure, and table 3-2 lists the domains within each relation. It should be noted that the relational data base used in this section is developed after examining the queries that will be made against the data base. In the last section of this chapter, the relational data base that would result from an automatic CODASYL-to-relational schema converter is described.

Using the relational terminology,[1] the data base consists of relations and domains, which correspond respectively to CODASYL record types

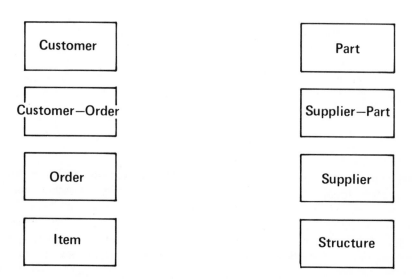

Figure 3-2. Relational Data Base Structure.

Table 3–2
Relational Data Base Relation Types

Customer	Part
Customer number	Part number
Customer name	Part description
Address	Date last transaction
Credit rating	Date stock taken
	Inventory at stock
	Inventory current
Customer order	Discount code
Customer number	Reorder point
Order number	
	Supplier Part
Order	Supplier number
Order number	Part number
Ship to address	Cost
Date of order	Price
Date closed	Delay
Value	
	Supplier
Item	Supplier number
Item number	Supplier name
Order number	
Dates created	*Structure*
Dates changed	Part number
Dates closed	Quantity
Dates required	
Dates shipped	
Part number	
Quantity	
Price unit	
Price extended	

and items. To maintain certain desirable mathematical characteristics, how-ever, a relational system may use several different relations rather than a single record type to describe a particular entity type, as with a CODASYL system. Relations also may be used to indicate a relationship between different types of entities in addition to describing a particular entity type. For example, a data base may contain a customer relation and an order relation as well as an explicit customer–order relation linking the two types of entities.

Relations have three important characteristics. First, since there cannot be identical rows, each record in the relation must have a unique or primary key. Second, the order of the rows is insignificant; that is, a sorted order is not maintained. Finally, every domain consists of a nondecomposable value.

A relation is simply a table of values. Each row, called a *tuple,* describes a specific entity or specific aspect of an entity. The columns are the domains or attributes of the entity and describe or identify a specific attribute. Any combination of domains which uniquely identifies the entity is called a *candidate key,* any one of which can be designated as the primary key. For example, customer number is the primary key of the customer relation and order number is the primary key of the order relation. For the customer–order relation linking these two, the two candidate keys are order number and the concatenation of the customer number and the order number. In the example data base, this combination is defined as the *primary key.*

Different relations are linked together or related through common domains. If the common domain is the primary key in one relation, then it is referred to as a foreign key in another relation. For example, order number is the primary key in the order relation but a foreign key in the item relation. If, for example, a query requires information about both an order and one of its items, then the order relation and the item relation are identified through the common order number. In a CODASYL data base, this relationship is provided by the set definition and is usually implemented with pointers linking the appropriate owner and member records.

Most of the characteristics of an item in the CODASYL data base apply to the domains in a relational system. The domains have names, lengths, and sets or ranges of acceptable values. The most obvious distinction is that CODASYL data items can be repeated but relational domains cannot. For example, a CODASYL customer record may have a repeating item identifying his orders, with as many entries as orders. The relational equivalent is a separate customer–order relation with one tuple for each customer–order pair. The disadvantage of this approach is that some of the data, that is, customer number, are repeated in each record or tuple. On the other hand, one advantage is that the relation's length is fixed and, therefore, usually easier to process. A more important advantage, though, is that if certain conditions are met, certain update problems are eliminated.

One example of a special type of update problem occurs in CODASYL when automatic sets are present. In the example data base, the customer–order set is automatic; therefore, every order must have a corresponding customer record. When a customer record is eliminated, then all the corresponding order records must also be eliminated. Thus the deletion of a single customer record also may require the deletion of many order records.

A corresponding problem occurs for insertion. It is impossible to add an order record unless there already is a corresponding customer record. Another example of these special cases is when modifying a record, a change to one must be propagated to many records. This situation would arise, for example, if the price of an item were included in both the part relation and the item relation. In this case, a simple request to change the price of a part would require not only changing a tuple in the part relation, but also all the tuples in the item relation involving the modified part. In fact, much of the difficulty in processing the last transaction, the one in which the price was changed after a certain date, is caused by this update problem. If the price were stored only in the part record and derived in all the other records, this transaction would be much easier to process. Those other transactions which require item and price data, however, would become more complex.

Relational systems propose to eliminate these update problems through a concept called "normalization".[2] While a CODASYL record can have repeating items for repeated attributes, a normalized relation cannot. This elimination of repeating items results in a first normal form (1NF). If, in addition, all the domains in the relation are functionally dependent on the key, the relation is in second normal form (2NF). Some of the domains in the relation, however, also may be dependent on other domains in addition to the key. For example, the item record in the example CODASYL data base includes item number, part number, and price. Although price is functionally dependent on item number, the dependence is indirect through part number. This indirect or transitive dependence is what creates the modification problems. This can be avoided if an additional restriction is included such that the domains are functionally dependent on only the primary key of the relation. This additional restriction results in mutually independent domains, and the relation is in third normal form (3NF). Thus, when a tuple is modified, added, or deleted, normalization should ensure that changes are made only to that single tuple. Ideally, this would result in processing only one tuple. Complex validation rules in the schema, however, may still require additional tuples, perhaps even in different relations.

Although the relational approach advocates maintaining the data base in third normal form to eliminate these special problems, it is typically impossible to check for all the conditions required to maintain this form. Therefore, a restriction may be imposed on the data base that the DBMS cannot maintain. An alternative approach, one used in many CODASYL DBMSs, is to explicitly state the possible restrictions and force the DBMS to maintain them. These restrictions frequently correspond to actual constraints in the real world, which the data base is supposed to be modeling. For example, most companies will not accept an order if they do not have corresponding information on the customer.

Operations on a relational data base may be specified in either a relational algebra or a relational calculus, corresponding to a low- or high-level query language. The relational calculus specifies the desired output of the query and allows the DBMS to select the appropriate method to obtain the results. A relational algebra query must specify not only the output, but also the method to obtain it. All the arguments favoring a high-level query language apply in evaluating relational calculus versus relational algebra languages.

Relational operations may be classified by their handling of a single relation or by more complex treatment of multiple relations. The basic operations on a single relation include selection, projection, modification, addition, deletion, division, set union, set intersection, and set difference. Selection identifies the desired tuples in a relation by specifying the values of certain domains within the relation. If a value of the primary key domain is specified, only a single record or no records are selected. If the primary key is not one of the domains specified, however, many records may be selected.

Projection identifies the domains of interest within the selected tuples. When multiple records are selected, the elimination of some domains by the projection operation may leave duplicate entries among the partial tuples that remain. Therefore, there are two types of projection—one in which the duplicates have been eliminated, and one in which they are included.

A modification operation changes the value of a domain in an existing tuple. Addition and deletion are relatively simple because the relations are of fixed length and the tuples are not maintained in any (sorted) order.

Division, intersection, union, and difference are four other operations that are sometimes included in relational data base processing. Division is a binary operation on two relations that results in a new relation. It is useful for answering such queries as "List all orders that contain both part a and part b." The remaining operations are set theoretic operations that also operate on two relations to produce a third. In each case, the relations used as operands must have at least one common domain.

The primary operation on multiple relations, the "join," is the relational equivalent to the set definition in the CODASYL data bases. Given two relations which have a common domain, the join combines the tuples of each relation where the values of the common domain are equal. In principle, a more general join can be defined as combining tuples when the common domains are related in some specified way, that is, equal, not equal, greater than, and so on. The join is a very complex operation because joining two relations of sizes M and N is generally of $M \times N$ complexity.

As described, the "full join" concatenates domains from both relations. A simpler "half join" presents only the domains from one of the relations as its output. The other relation's common domain values are used to select the required tuples from the first domain. The half join provides a relational means of dynamically materializing specific set occurrences. The full join, in one operation, materializes all the set occurrences for the specified type of set.

The relational equivalent of the example manufacturing data base consists of eight relations. The six basic relations are customer, order, item, part, supplier, and structure. Two additional relations, customer–order, created to provide a link between customers and their orders, and supplier–part, created to provide a link between parts and their suppliers, are also present. Although these relationships could have been implemented with the customer number as a foreign key in the order relation and part number as a foreign key in the supplier relation, separate relations were created simply to illustrate this method of linkage. Thus this example relational data base is not an optimal design, rather it is intended to aid in the illustration of the various relational operations on the typical set of transactions previously established.

The remainder of this section describes how a relational DBMS would process the same set of transactions described for a CODASYL DBMS. The transactions, already in a high–level, content–based form, are described as being processed with the basic relational operations executing on associative hardware. This approach is the most illuminating because most of the data base computer architectures, at least at the logical level, postulate this capability. A description of these operations in terms of a physical implementation on conventional hardware would be very similar to the previously described CODASYL approach and therefore not very useful.

List the address for customer *ABC*.

For this simple transaction, the customer relation is scanned to locate customer *ABC*, and when the appropriate tuple is located, the address is listed. Even though the primary key is specified, a sophisticated access method to locate the desired tuple is not required. Instead, the entire relation is scanned and the customer identifier is examined until the correct tuple is found. The only benefit of knowing that the primary key is being used is that the scan can stop when a single tuple is found because there cannot be another tuple with the same primary key value. Because of the underlying physical implementation, however, the DBMS may recognize that the customer identifier is the primary key, and therefore, the DBMS will hash or index into the relation.

List all the order numbers for customer *ABC*.

This query is answered by first scanning the customer–order relation and selecting all the tuples for customer *ABC*. Then, by projecting over the order domain all the order numbers for customer *ABC* are listed. Although similar to the previous query in that a simple search of a single relation is all that is necessary, this one requires examining the entire relation because any number of tuples could be selected.

List all the items in order 1234.

In the relational approach, this query is identical to the previous one, requiring a search of a single relation and resulting in the selection of any number of tuples. For this query, the item relation is first searched for all tuples with order number 1234, and the required data are then listed for the selected items.

List all the items in customer *ABC*'s latest order.

This transaction requires processing three different relations. First, the customer–order relation is scanned, and all the tuples for customer *ABC* are selected. This is followed by a projection because only the order numbers are needed. Selection is then performed on the order relation to find the tuples for these orders. The DBMS must then examine the date of each of these orders to determine the latest one. Finally, the item relation is scanned to select all the tuples with that order number.

This process involves extracting a domain common to two relations, using one relation to select the desired values and then using these values to select tuples from the other relation. In effect, this operation is dynamically materializing sets, the set of all orders for a customer and the set of all items within an order. This is, in fact, the relational join operation. An alternative description of handling this query is as follows: Join the customer–order and the order relation where the customer number in the customer–order relation is *ABC*. Select the tuple in this new temporary relation with the latest date and join it with the item relation using order number as the common field. This locates all the tuples for the items in the latest order.

The operations for this transaction actually involve a series of half joins rather than the more complex full join, which is, in general, a many-to-many operation and requires domains from both relations. The distinguishing feature of the half join is that only the common field is required from the first relation, while all the data domains come from the second relation. In effect, the first relation is simply used to build a selection expression. The command to join the order and item relations on order number, where the order number is for the latest order, is equivalent to: "Given a set of order tuples, select the one with the latest date, then take its order number and select all the item tuples with the same order number."

Reduce the inventory level of part *xyz* by 100.

This transaction causes the DBMS to scan the order relation until part *xyz* is located. Because part number is the primary key of the part relation, the scan can once again end as soon as the unique tuple is found. The tuple is then locked, the inventory level changed, and the tuple unlocked.

Add new customer *DEF* to the data base.

This relatively simple insertion is performed by locking the relation, adding the new tuple, and then unlocking the relation. Because relations are not maintained in an ordered sequence, a search does not have to be performed to find the proper place to insert the new tuple. At this point, however, a validity check may be desirable. Because the customer number is the primary key and uniquely identifies the tuple, a scan of the entire relation is needed to ensure that the customer number for the new tuple is not already in the relation.

Add new order (number 4567) for customer *ABC*.

In principle, this insert is as simple as the previous one if the data base is maintained in third normal form. The relation is locked, the tuple for the new order added, and the relation unlocked. Subsequent inserts add the items for the order to the data base. As with the last example, the relation does not have to be searched to find where to insert the new order, but it should be scanned to ensure that the primary key (order number) is unique.

In typical manufacturing environments, additional validity constraints frequently exist and therefore should be specified to be maintained by the DBMS. For example, a company may have a policy that it must have certain information on a customer before it will accept his order. By specifying this to the DBMS, it could check the customer relation to ensure that the customer is already in the data base before inserting the new order. If there is already a customer–order tuple, then the order tuple is simply inserted as described earlier. If there is only a customer tuple and not a customer–order tuple, the corresponding customer–order tuple must also be created and inserted. If there were no tuple for the customer in the customer relation, however, then the insertion of the order should be rejected even though the insertion would still conform to the rules for maintaining third normal form. The case of having a tuple in the customer–order relation but not in the customer relation would not be possible if the customer relation were checked before making the insertion in the customer–order relation.

Add an additional item to order 1234.

The processing of this transaction is similar to the previous one except that different relations are used. Although it is not necessary to maintain third normal form, checks should be made to ensure that there is an order to which to add the item and that the part being ordered (stock number) is a part in the inventory. This requires scanning both the order relation and the part relation to ensure that the tuples with the necessary primary keys exist.

Delete part *xyz* from the inventory.

For this transaction, the DBMS must lock the part relation, scan it to find part *xyz*, delete the part, and unlock the relation. Because part number is a primary key, the scan can stop as soon as the tuple is found. If the data base is maintained in third normal form, the transaction is then complete. Even if this were the only part provided by a particular supplier, the supplier tuple with all the information on the supplier would remain in the data base. Leaving this supplier information in the data base appears reasonable because other parts may be ordered from this supplier at some later date.

In the actual application, this simple deletion still may cause serious problems. For example, a company does not normally accept orders for parts it does not carry. This situation can be avoided by checking the stock number before an item is inserted to ensure that the part being ordered is included in the inventory. Although this check covers future orders for the deleted part, there still may be unfilled orders for that part. Therefore, the item relation must be scanned prior to deleting the part to find any items requesting it. If there are none, then the part can be deleted without any side effects. Otherwise, either the delete must be rejected or some other action must be taken for each of those items. An example would be to notify the customer that the item is no longer carried and will have to be ordered elsewhere. From a practical point of view, then, it seems unreasonable to simply delete the part, even if the data base is designed to allow it, and thus ignore these possible side effects.

How many orders are there?

This query simply requires a count of the tuples in either the customer-order relation or the order relation because each relation has one tuple for each order.

Calculate the total value of all orders.

This transaction requires scanning the order relation and summing the value of each order.

What is the average order value?

This transaction is a combination of the previous two. During a scan of the order relation, both a count of the number of tuples and a sum of the value of the orders is built. When the scan is completed, the average is calculated and returned to the user.

Add 10 percent to the price of part *xyz* for all orders after June 1, 1979.

In response to this, the DBMS scans the part relation to locate the tuple for part *xyz*, locks the tuple, modifies the price, and then unlocks the tuple. If the data base were in third normal form, then only the tuple in the part relation is changed because only this relation contains the price. In this example relational data base, however, the price is a domain in the item relation as well as in the part relation. Because the price is directly dependent on the stock number (part number) and not on the item number, the relation is not in third normal form. To improve the performance of the other transactions, the data base is in second normal form. This form requires scanning the item relation to locate all items involving that part. Each of the items, ordered after the effective date and not already containing the new price, are locked and then modified to change both the item price and date changed values.

In addition, some order tuples also have to be modified. The value for the order is revised by joining the order and item relations on the order–number domain for every item tuple which was changed. The selected order tuples are then locked, modified to reflect the new item price, and unlocked. Once again, the concept of third normal form suggests not including price or value data in the order record to avoid this complexity. If this were done, processing of both the item and the part relation would be required each time a value of an order is needed.

3–4. The Converted Data Base

The special–purpose data base computers that have been designed to date offer the largest performance improvements to relational data bases. Currently, however, many times more CODASYL than relational data bases exist in production invironments. With the large investments in existing data bases and applications, a major conversion is certainly unpalatable if not unthinkable. To protect this investment and still offer major performance improvement requires sophisticated conversion support. One approach, conversion from a CODASYL to a relational data base, is discussed in this section.

Conversion may involve either changing the data base, the applications, or both. Because of the high labor costs involved, it is necessary to automate as much of the conversion effort as possible. Automation, though, is a more viable option for converting the data base than the applications. In all likelihood, the latter would be a very labor-intensive activity, especially if they were written in a low-level data manipulation language.

Given that most current data bases have a CODASYL structure, one conversion approach is to allow the user to issue relational transactions which are then converted into the equivalent CODASYL data manipulation language. This approach leaves current applications and data bases unchanged and affects only new applications. From the user's perspective, this approach provides some improvements through the use of a high-level language with his current CODASYL system. It does not really solve, however, the performance problem of a CODASYL data base on relational data base computer architectures.

Fortunately, a second conversion approach will resolve the performance issue. Given a CODASYL data base and a mixture of high- and low-level transactions, the data base is converted. This new relational data base allows both new relational transactions and the previous high- and low-level CODASYL transactions to be processed without user intervention. The two previous sections described two data bases, a CODASYL one and a relational one and a common set of transactions against them. The only apparent difference was in processing the transactions by the two DBMSs. This section describes a single data base which allows either a CODASYL or a relational application to process the transaction.

The section first discusses the major conversion issue: the implementation of set relationships. Next, there is a description of conversion from the traditional CODASYL data base to a common data base form. This conversion requires the specification of both set membership and sequence. The last part of the section discuss how the example transactions are processed against this common data base for both CODASYL and relational applications.

In a CODASYL data base, record types are related by defining sets that are implemented with pointers. These pointers are either embedded within the records or stored separately in pointer arrays. The sets are defined and their implementation method specified when the data base is initially defined. Within a relational data base, various relations can be dynamically linked by joining them on a domain common to both relations. Not having pointers increases the flexibility of the system by allowing arbitrary ad hoc transactions to form new relations by joining any two relations having common domains. A performance penalty, however, is incurred when used with conventional computer architectures. A compromise approach taken by System R is to use pointers as the underlying implementation of the anticipated links and to dynamically construct additional sets of pointers to implement the unanticipated ad hoc linkages when necessary.[3] This approach provides the desired flexibility, with a performance degradation occurring only with those ad hoc transactions requiring unanticipated joins. With an associative or parallel data base computer architecture, however, the performance benefits can be obtained without the performance penalties of maintaining sets of pointers.

The CODASYL schema defines the record types and sets within the data base. When the data base is converted into the common relational format, every record type becomes a relation. A new relation must be created, however, if there is a repeating item or group in the record. This new relation contains the record key and one occurrence of the repeating group. For example, if the customer record contains order number as a repeating group, then the new relation would simply contain customer number and one order number. Each customer record gives rise to as many tuples in the new relation as there were orders for the customer.

All the information defining the data items within the record remain unchanged. The member records of every set, however, are expanded with the key of the owner record. Therefore, if a record is a member of n sets, then n additional fields that specify the key of each owner record are added to the record. Moreover, these keys may be propagated through any number of levels. The application of these procedures is illustrated in the example data base in the common format of figure 3–3 and table 3–3.

In the common relational format, there is a customer relation with customer number as its key and an order relation with order number as its key. In addition, because there is a relationship between customers and orders, the customer number is pushed down into the order record as a foreign key. If all the orders for a particular customer are required, then the selection

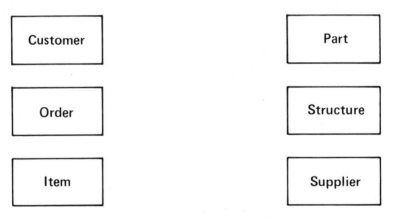

Figure 3–3. Converted Data Base Structure.

Table 3–3
Converted Data Base Relation Types

Customer	*Part*
Customer number	Part number
Customer name	Part description
Address	Date last transaction
Credit rating	Date stock taken
Order numbers	Inventory at stock
	Inventory current
	Discount code
Order	Reorder point
Order number	Supplier number
(Customer number)	Cost
[Customer order	Price
set sequence field]	Delay
Ship to address	
Date of order	
Date closed	*Supplier*
Value	Supplier number
	Supplier name
	(Part number)
	[Part supplier set
Item	sequence field]
Item number	
(Order number)	
(Customer number)	
[Order item set	*Structure*
sequence field]	Part number
[Part item set	(Part number of used by set
sequence field]	owner)
Date created	(Part number of where used set
Date changed	owner)
Date closed	[Used by set sequence field]
Date required	[Where used set sequence
Date shipped	field]
Part number	Quantity
Quantity	
Price unit	
Price extended	

Note: ( ) = Key of owner records pushed down to members.
    [ ] = Sequencing field used to maintain set ordering.

can be entirely performed using only the order relation. If both customer and order information are needed, however, the appropriate set can be dynamically constructed by joining the customer and order relations on customer number.

In a similar manner, order number is pushed down to the item records at the next level. At this point, storage versus processing time tradeoffs should be considered. Every additional level or set into which owner keys are pushed down increases the redundant storage. On the other hand, relationships of records through several sets, for example, customers to items, can be processed faster if the keys are pushed down through all the sets. In the example data base, if the keys are pushed down through only one set, then the only way to link customers to items is through the order records. If the keys are pushed down through all the sets, however, then item records can be directly linked to the corresponding customer records without going through the order records.

At this point, it will be assumed that the keys are pushed down through all the sets. This approach requires, then, only the data base definition or schema and therefore can be automated fairly easily. By careful analysis of how the data base is used, though, the data base administrator could explicitly decide which keys to push down and how far to push them. The inclusion of data base usage as well as the data base definition in the conversion algorithm results in a more efficient design for the converted data base.

Thus the example converted data base is built by pushing down the customer number into the order records. Each item record also has its key augmented with the key of its owner (an order record). Therefore, each item relation now contains its key, an item number, and a concatenated order number and customer number, forming the key for its owner order record. In addition, the item relation is augmented with a part number because it is also a member of a set with parts as the owner. Finally, the structure relation is augmented with two part numbers because it is a member of two sets, both of which have a part record as the owner.

Implementing sets by pushing down owner keys has two conflicting effects. It eliminates the need for pointers, thereby reducing the size of the data base. On the other hand, it results in the redundant storage of many keys that normally would expand the data base. Actually, only part of this redundancy increases the size of the data base because some of these keys are already redundantly stored in the CODASYL system. (Note: The CODASYL schema in table 3-1 shows that the customer number, order number, and part number keys already are pushed down to the member records. Therefore, for the record types used in this example, the conversion to the common relational form actually results in a reduction in storage because its only effect is the elimination of the pointers.)

In addition to identifying the owner and member record types, the

CODASYL set definition also specifies the set mode and order. The mode specification can be ignored because it selects one of two physical implementations, neither of which is applicable to the common relational model.

The CODASYL set order is the remaining piece of critical information that must be treated. The user of the set expects to retrieve the members in a specified order. Therefore, the equivalent relational data base must be able to reproduce this ordering. The possible orderings are first, last, next, prior, and sorted with duplicates (if allowed), either first or last. All these orderings, except sorted without duplicates, require an additional sequence field within the record. This field is added when the data base is converted to allow unconverted low-level CODASYL applications to execute with the converted relational data base. This new field is maintained by and is accessable only to the DBMS and not to the users of the data base. Although these sequence numbers are required only for the CODASYL applications, they also must be provided and maintained for records added by relational transactions. Otherwise, the CODASYL transactions will not be able to process records added by the relational transactions and the data base will no longer be the same for the two interfaces.

A sequencing also must be applied to all the records of a particular type, regardless of their particular set occurrence. For example, there must be a single sequence for all order records as well as for the orders of a specific customer, because there are times when all the order records must be traversed independently of their owners. First and last are positional orderings that specify where a new member is to be inserted in the set. To implement this ordering, an additional field is needed in each member record to time stamp or sequence the members as they are added to the set. When this type of set is retrieved, then, it is ordered on the basis of this additional field. Duplicate key values do not create additional complications for this type of ordering.

Next and prior are positional orderings that are dependent on the current position of the application in traversing the set. Next and prior ordering force an insert to be made immediately after or before the current record. Because a set must be traversed in the same order, the sequencing field required to allow first or last ordering is also needed here. Time stamps, which were sufficient for first and last ordering, however, cannot be used in this case because an insertion is allowed at any point within the set and not just at one of the two ends. Therefore, a sparse sequence numbering must be used to provide for the insertion of additional records between any two current members of the set. Too many inserts at a particular point would require resequencing of the entire set.

Sorted order based on a specified key is easy to maintain if there are no duplicates, because the key domain is already part of the relation. If duplicates are allowed, however, then the new record must be inserted either first or last, that is, either before or after the current record with the same key value. This requires the same additional sequence field as that for the normal first or last ordering case.

A relation is not normally maintained in a sorted order, but the selected records or the entire relation is appropriately sorted for output. While this increases the processing requirements for retrieving a sorted set, it reduces both the storage requirement and the insertion processing because it is not necessary to maintain pointers to link the set members in the proper order.

The remainder of this section describes the operation of the transactions on the example data base maintained in the common format of figure 3-3 and Table 3-3.

List the address for customer *ABC*.

In answer to this request, the DBMS scans the customer relation for the tuple with the value *ABC* in the primary key. This procedure satisfies the high-level query from a relational system as well as a low-level CODASYL query because additional application processing is not required to complete the operation.

List all the order numbers for customer *ABC*.

Because the customer number is pushed down into the order relation, the orders for a specific customer from a relational system can be identified simply by scanning the order relation.

A low-level CODASYL application, using a series of commands, first selects the customer record in a manner similar to that for the previous transaction and returns it to the application. The user then requests the first order record in the set of orders for that customer. A series of GET NEXT commands is issued by the application to retrieve the order number for each order. Thus the DBMS appears to traverse the set and extract the order number from each record.

To improve performance in this case, the DBMS retrieves all the order records for the customer as soon as the first member of the set is requested. Although the entire set is retrieved, the DBMS sends the application only the first record in order to remain compatible with the CODASYL application. The remaining members of the set are sent one at a time to the application in response to each GET NEXT command. This anticipatory fetching of the entire set appears to be very costly in those cases in which the user needs only the one specified record. With associative processing, however, the time to identify and fetch the entire set differs insignificantly from the time required to fetch a single record from the set. This is especially true when compared with the time to actually fetch the records one at a time for each GET NEXT command. Therefore, even if many times entire sets are unnecessarily retrieved to obtain just a single record, there is still a significant performance improvement on the average.

Given that the entire set is fetched, there is still a question of the order in which to present the records to the user. The basic procedures were explained previously in the discussion of set ordering. The set of the selected tuples in the relation is ordered on either a key value or a sequence number depending on how the set is defined. In this specific case, the set ordering is first. Therefore, the set is ordered, that is, tuples are presented, on the basis of the sequence number or time stamp inserted in the new field that was created when the data base was converted.

List all the items in order 1234.

The relational and CODASYL versions of this query are processed similarly to their corresponding descriptions in the previous one. For the CODASYL query, the set is sorted by item number in this case.

List all the items in customer ABC's latest order.

For the high-level language request, the processing of the example data base in the common format is the same as for the pure relational one. The order relation is scanned for all the tuples for customer *ABC* and the latest order is determined. Then the item relation is scanned for all the tuples with that order number.

Processing this same transaction from a low-level CODASYL application is much more difficult because the application requests only one record at a time. In this case, a command is first issued to retrieve the record for customer *ABC*, an operation previously described. Although this step is necessary for the low-level application, it would not be if the application were converted. Next, the application requests the first order in the set of orders for this customer, but the DBMS retrieves the entire set of all orders for this customer. Because the set is ordered first, the DBMS has embedded a new sequence field in the order record. The set of orders which has been retrieved is then ordered on this sequence number and the first-order record is returned to the user. The application examines this record and determines the date of the order. The application then traverses the set by issuing a series of GET NEXT requests and identifies and saves the latest order. With each GET NEXT request, the DBMS just passes the record with the next lowest sequence number and does not actually retrieve any more data. Once the latest order is identified, the process is repeated to list the items for that order. The application requests the first member of the set and then traverses the rest of the set, one record at a time. Meanwhile, the DBMS retrieves the entire set, orders it by sequence number, and sends the appropriate records to the application as it traverses the set.

Reduce the inventory level of part *xyz* by 100.

For this transaction, the part relation is scanned to find the tuple for *xyz*, and then the tuple is locked, modified, and unlocked. This operation is the same for both types of requests because an explicit series of substeps is not required for the low–level CODASYL application.

Add new customer *DEF* to the data base.

In this case, the customer relation is locked, the new tuple added, and the relation unlocked. As discussed previously in section 3–3, a check should be made to ensure that there is no customer with the same number in the relation, because customer number is the primary key of the relation. If there already is one, the new tuple should be rejected. The low–level command for this insert is processed similarly because customer records are only owners of a set and not members and therefore do not cause an ordering problem.

Add new order (number 4567) for customer *ABC*.

This and the following transaction illustrate the added complication that arises when set members are involved and an ordering must be maintained. For this first transaction, two checks should be made before inserting. One ensures that the order number in the order relation is unique, and the other ensures that the customer tuple in the customer relation exists.

The insertion of records which are members of sets is slightly more complicated than the insertion of records which are only owners. Because the set ordering must be maintained for all the inserts regardless of whether they were initiated by a CODASYL or a relational transaction, the DBMS must add a sequencing field to the record. With the set ordering first, the sequence number of the current first record in the set can be incremented by one and used as the sequence number for the new order. It should be noted, however, that some applications may want to traverse all the orders rather than just the orders for a specific customer. Therefore, a second sequence number should be constructed for all the orders and not just for the orders for a particular customer.

Add an additional item to order 1234.

For this second more complicated transaction, a check should be made to ensure that order 1234 exists and that the item number is not duplicated.

If the insertion can be made, the item relation is locked, the tuple is inserted, and the relation is unlocked for either the relational or the CODASYL application. Because the CODASYL set that relates orders and items is maintained in sorted order, additional fields do not have to be added to the record for this set. The item record is also a member of a set that relates item and part records and is maintained also in sorted order. If this other set were being maintained in another order (for example, first), then a sequence field would have to be added for that set.

Delete part *xyz* from the inventory.

In response to this request, the part relation is scanned to locate the tuple for *xyz*, the relation is locked, the tuple is deleted, and the relation is unlocked. This completes the transaction processing if only relational transactions were used. If this was not the case, additional steps are necessary to maintain the consistency of the data base for CODASYL transactions. In the example data base, the part record is an owner of one set of items and an owner of two sets relating it to structures. In CODASYL, when the owner of an automatic set is deleted, all the members of the set also must be deleted. Therefore, consistency is maintained by deleting all the related item and structure records before the transaction is completed.

How many orders are there?

To determine the answer for a relational query, the DBMS scans and counts the number of tuples in the order relation. A similar operation is performed for the low-level CODASYL query, with the exception that the application traverses the set of orders with a series of GET NEXT commands. The entire set is retrieved when the first record is requested, and the succeeding records are produced as each GET NEXT command is issued. A high-level CODASYL query functions as the relational query in that the DBMS rather than the application traverses the records.

Calculate the total value of all orders.

This transaction is processed like the previous one, with one exception. As the tuples are scanned, the DBMS or the application sums the total value of the orders instead of counting the tuples.

What is the average order value?

This transaction is similar to the previous two. The order relation is scanned, and the DBMS or the application counts the number of tuples and accumulates the value of the orders. When the scan of the relation is complete, the average value is calculated.

Add 10 percent to the price of part *xyz* for all orders after June 1, 1979.

In addition to changing the price in the part record, which is the same as the previous transaction that changed the inventory level, this transaction requires changing the price in all the item tuples dated after the effective date. For the high-level transaction, the item relation is scanned and all those tuples with both the given part number and dated later than the effective date are selected. These tuples are then locked, the price is changed, and then the tuples are unlocked. For the low-level transaction, the set linking items to parts is traversed. As described previously, the entire set is obtained when the first member is requested and the remaining members are passed to the application, one at a time, in the proper sequence as successive GET NEXT commands are issued.

Summary

Three different approaches, CODASYL, relational, and converted CODASYL-relational, were discussed in this chapter in terms of a typical manufacturing application. In chapter 4, a set of criteria involving performance, cost, range, and evolvability is established. These criteria and the transaction types in this chapter can be applied to the data base computer architectures of chapter 5 or any new ones that are developed, and an indepth evaluation can be obtained.

Notes

1. E.F. Codd, "A Relational Model of Data for Large Shared Data Banks," *Communications of the ACM* 13, No. 6, June 1970, pp. 377–387.

2. E.F. Codd, "Normalized Data Base Structure: A Brief Tutorial," *Proceedings 1971 ACM-SIGFIDET Workshop in Data Description, Access and Control,* November 1971, pp. 1–17.

3. M.M. Astrahan et al., "System R: A Relational Data Base Management System," *Computer 12,* No. 5, May 1979, pp. 42–48.

4

Evaluation Criteria for Data Base Computers

Chapter 2 identified those user/application, system, and administration functions that would be performed by a data base management system independent of a data base computer (DBC). With these requirements defined, there is now a basis for evaluating various hardware architectural alternatives and for determining which functions should be included in the data base computer and which functions should remain on the host or other system elements. The evaluation criteria listed in this chapter are defined and their importance explained. Suggestions are made for determining or measuring the factors to be evaluated.

The following four sections describe the evaluation criteria. Section 4-1 deals with performance measures. From the operational point of view, this includes throughput, response time, and recovery metrics. Included is a procedure for evaluating the operational performance of a data base computer with respect to CODASYL data bases. From the application design viewpoint, performance translates to ease of use and degree of conversion involved.

The cost factors, both one-time and recurring, involved with a data base computer are described in section 4-2. Also included is a discussion of the importance of hardware-software cost tradeoffs.

Every data base user has his or her own set of needs and concerns regarding data base operations. Secton 4-3 suggests a collection of factors that should be considered in determining how large and how well a group could be served by a data base computer. Modularity, view support, functional capabilities, system configurations, and the other factors listed in this section, though, must be balanced against the cost metrics of section 4-2 and the estimated DBC usage in evaluating their inclusion in a DBC or DBC system.

Section 4-4 considers those factors which are used to evaluate the period of usefulness or product life cycle of a data base computer. The emphasis is on the impact of new technologies in the areas of data base computer improvement, limitations, and obsolescence.

4-1. Performance

Performance criteria fall into two broad areas—operational and application development. The operational criteria are used to measure the system performance for a particular application or mix of applications. The application development criteria measure the complexity involved in developing an application that will execute on a system incorporating a data base computer.

The basic tradeoff in the performance area is between operational performance and application development. From the hardware and software perspective, efficiency is obtained by tailoring the system to a specific application, although this greatly complicates application development. A generalized system providing high–level facilities is much easier to use but less efficient than a specifically tailored system with only low–level facilities. Comparing the hardware costs of a computer system with the personnel costs provides one metric for making this tradeoff.

All the performance criteria are dependent on the data base computer architecture, the basic data model it supports, and the specific application, that is, data base structure and usage. Therefore, different architectures must be evaluated against a common data base and a set of transactions.

The evaluation of the various architectures requires three types of information on the selected benchmark. First, there should be a description of the types of applications, queries, and updates in the benchmark and their frequency. Second, there should be a description of the data base structure, that is, the various record types or relations within the data base. A relational version of the data base is important because the relational approach is the one most compatible with many of the DBC architectures, and it appears that the relational approach will come into widespread use in the future. Finally, for comparisons, a comparable CODASYL or network–structured data base should be defined, both in its conventional form and in the form in which it would be used on the DBC. In other words, the network–structured data base on conventional hardware should be compared with two alternatives using the DBC. The first alternative is a relational data base on the DBC; that is, the data base has been converted from a network to a relational form. In addition, some indication of the complexity of this conversion should be provided. The second alternative is to use the DBC with a converted, but not redesigned, network–structured data base.

Operational Performance

The three parts of this subsection consider the operational performance factors in the evaluation. The first part identifies and defines the actual criteria to be used and their importance. The second part describes the methodology to be used to measure the criteria. The third part explicitly compares the DBC approach to the current CODASYL approach.

Criteria. Within the operational-performance area there are two sets of tradeoffs. First, there is the traditional tradeoff between throughput and response time. Up to a point, the additional system overhead to keep multiple tasks active, that is, to improve response time, is acceptable. This is especially true when the additional overhead consists of the use of otherwise unavailable or idle system resources. When the overhead begins to reduce the time available for application processing, however, throughput is sacrificed for response time. Another factor to be considered in this tradeoff is that the system software to support such concurrency is more complex and difficult to maintain. Based on analysis of various applications,[1] equal weight should be attached to the throughput and the response-time criteria.

The second tradeoff involves backup and recovery. Measurements must be made of recovery time and of transaction overhead time spent in producing the backup information necessary to the recovery procedure. The additional processing required and the additional data stored by the backup procedures result in greater overhead and a corresponding reduction in throughput, response time, or both. On the other hand, more extensive backup procedures ensure faster completion of the actual recovery. Backup actions must be taken for every transaction. Recovery, however, needs to be done only when there is a failure. Therefore, the determination of the tasks that are, or can be, shifted from the backup to the recovery procedures is required for the tradeoff. The upper bound on this is how long the user can accept having his data base "down" and unavailable during recovery.

These tradeoffs suggest three operational evaluation criteria. The first two—throughput and response time—are relatively straightforward. Throughput provides a measure of the amount of work the system can do. It is determined by counting the number of transactions or jobs that can be processed in a given period of time. Because throughput depends on the complexity of the transactions, all the alternatives must be evaluated against a common benchmark. Response time is primarily an on-line or transaction-oriented criteria. It is determined by measuring the time between entering the last character of a message and receiving the first character of the response. Turnaround time is the equivalent criterion for batch applications. Response time is also dependent on transaction complexity.

The third criterion, involving backup and recovery, is more complex. First, the recovery time must be determined, that is, the period of time the data base or parts of it are unavailable following a failure or error. Second, the overhead paid by each transaction to support the system's backup and recovery procedures must be found. An additional complication is that there are several different types of problems or failures from which to recover. For one, the system must be able to recover from a partial or total loss of the data base. It also must be able to return the data base to a previous state either to remove the effects of erroneous entries or to eliminate the effects of a deadlocked transaction.

Methodology. Many methods—including memory cycle time, add time, instruction kernel times, benchmarks, and simulation—have been used to evaluate computer system performance. The operational performance of the architectural alternatives for a data base computer can be evaluated using two methodologies: benchmarking and simulation. First, the performance measurements for the network data base running on conventional hardware can be obtained using a data management system benchmark. Performance measures for the two DBC approaches, that is, a converted and a redesigned data base, can be obtained using a model of the various DBC architectures running the same data base activity profile as the benchmark. Because simulation is one of the few methods that can be used to evaluate the performance of complex systems before they are actually implemented, it must be used in this case for the DBC architectures. This requires using the data base of an application running on current equipment or defining a hypothetical data base and specifying a profile of activity or benchmark as described earlier. Second, models of the various DBC architectures can be formulated. The performance measurements and the precision desired are then used to determine the level of detail and complexity of the model.

The results provided by the simulation should include average throughput and response times for both the overall system and for each transaction type. Potential bottlenecks within the system, indicated by the length of time transactions spend in certain queues, also can be identified.

For this analysis, an analytical network queuing model rather than discrete-event simulation may be preferable for both theoretical and practical reasons.[2] Because the evaluation criteria require estimates of only the average system performance, the additional detail available using discrete-event simulation is not necessary. It is more important to be able to easily and quickly vary the data base activity profile than it is to be able to obtain detailed distribution statistics. Later more detailed studies may be used if any distribution statistics are desired. From a practical viewpoint, the analytical queuing network models are easier to develop and modify than the discrete-event simulation models. Also, the solutions using this approach usually require much less computer time. Therefore, the analytic approach, which allows greater exploration of various architectures, should be considered for evaluation purposes.

Backup and recovery criteria must be considered in two ways. The first is simply a determination that the architecture provides a way to recover from each of the identified problem types. The second type of criteria indirectly considers backup and recovery. It requires measuring how much overhead is involved in the backup procedures and how long the recovery takes. This is found by considering the effect of the backup and recovery procedures on the overall system throughput and response time, that is, comparing the performance of the system with no backup and recovery procedures to its performance with the complete procedures.

CODASYL DMS Comparison. Because of the parallelism involved in the search operations performed by a data base computer (DBC), many low-level transactions can be executed considerably faster on a DBC than on a conventional computer. This is achieved by retrieving a set of record occurrences with a given property at one time and temporarily placing this set in a fast random–access buffer. By keeping account of the information stored in this buffer, it is often possible to execute the essentially record–at–a–time statements by accessing the buffer instead of the relatively slower permanent data base storage. For example, it is possible to retrieve an entire set occurrence or all records within that set occurrence having certain specified properties. This information, stored in the buffer, can be used during the execution of a sequence of low–level statements. For example, examine the format 3, format 5, and format 6 FIND statements given in the DBTG report of April 1971.[3] Unfortunately, the statements do not allow some other kinds of search operations. For instance, to find all record occurrences of a given type that satisfy certain conditions (irrespective of the sets to which they belong), a host language (COBOL or PL/1) procedure has to be used. The search condition is separately specified in the host language. Thus a DBC cannot be used directly to retrieve only the restricted set of records.

The gain in speed achievable with the DBC is not merely dependent on its own processing power, but also on the characteristics of the data base and on the types of transactions commonly executed. This is so because these factors govern the amount of parallelism that can be effectively used on a DBC. Given a data base and a group of typical applications, the parameters to be measured are identified in this section to estimate the performance of a DBC with respect to that of a conventional computer. The parameters can be grouped into *static parameters*—those which are relatively unchanging, such as the schema definition, average number of occurrences per record type, and so on—and *dynamic parameters*—those which are determined by specific applications. The dynamic parameters can be measured directly from the abstract or high–level description of the applications or can be obtained by analysis of the actual transactions (such as benchmarks).

In a conventional implementation, the data base is divided into pages, each page being individually addressable and requiring a single data base access for retrieval or storage. All records (or record occurrences) within a given page have data base keys that belong to a particular range, because data base keys are determined by an area name, a page number, and an offset within the page. Records with location mode DIRECT are assigned arbitrary data base keys (within a given area) and, therefore, must be stored in specific pages. Records with location mode CALC are also stored in specific pages, except that two or more records with identical CALC keys will be placed in the same page whenever possible. Records with location mode VIA a set are frequently placed "near" to their owner records for performance reasons. Ordering of records in a set occurrence is maintained by the use of pointers instead of by physical ordering. During the execution of transactions, a page–sized buffer is used to store an entire page retrieved from the data base. If a page is requested that is already stored in the buffer, no further data base access is required.

In a content-based DBC implementation, pointers need not be used. Only one physical block (for example, a disk cylinder or a group of disk cylinders) can be accessed at a time. Hence there is a need for grouping or clustering of records and for keeping track of the whereabouts of these clusters. All records (or record occurrences) of a particular type are stored in as few blocks as possible, but this may still represent more than a single block. Therefore, all record occurrences of a given type are grouped with respect to the ranges in which their data base keys belong and clustered (secondarily) accordingly. The assignment of data base keys ensures that it is possible to identify the block number in which a record belongs if its location mode is DIRECT or CALC. It also ensures that all member records of a set occurrence are stored (almost always) in the same physical block if they are of the same record type and are declared to have a location mode VIA that set. In case the location mode is not VIA this set, then these member records will be returned in at most as many accesses as there are blocks required to store all occurrences of the given member record type. This is so because records are clustered primarily by their record type.

The location mode of the various record types determines the way they are normally accessed and the time required to access arbitrary occurrences of such record types. The static parameters needed in this case are

1. The number of different record types of each of the three location modes (DIRECT, CALC, and VIA sets).
2. The maximum, minimum, and average number of occurrences of record types having a given location mode (DIRECT, CALC, or VIA).

Most search operations on a CODASYL data base are carried out by navigating through sets. A number of other operations such as insertion of records into sets, removal of records from sets, storing records in the data base, and deletion of records from the data base require the traversal of sets. In order to estimate the time required to carry out such operations, what is needed are

1. The number of different "clustered" set types (those having one or

more member record types with location mode VIA the corresponding set).

2. The number of different "unclustered" set types.
3. The maximum and average number of member record types per set types.
4. The maximum, minimum, and average number of occurrences per set type.
5. The maximum, minimum, and average number of member record occurrences per set occurrence.

An application may sometimes need to scan all occurrences of a record type in order to find those which satisfy a given condition. This may be done by sequentially traversing all the areas in which that record type is stored. To estimate the time required in these operations what is needed are

1. The maximum, minimum, and average number of pages per area.
2. The number of areas in the data base.
3. The maximum and average number of areas in which all occurrences of a record type are stored.

CODASYL allows member records of a set occurrence to be logically ordered based on the values of certain data items used as sort keys. In case such sorted ordering is not important, then the set ordering is decided by procedural means (order being NEXT or PRIOR) or by the sequence in which records are inserted into a set occurrence (order being FIRST or LAST). Only one type of ordering is allowed on a set type, even though more than one sorted order can be maintained by means of address pointers. Thus, whenever necessary, procedural means are used to sort set occurrences if the required sort order is not the one originally defined on the set type. Most data base computers usually do not maintain sorted ordering, even if a set type is so defined. Set occurrences of such set types are sorted during retrieval. In order to determine the importance currently assigned to a single predefined sorted order, what is needed are

1. The number of set types with each type of ordering (FIRST, LAST, NEXT, PRIOR, or sorted).
2. The average, maximum, and minimum number of member record occurrences in each set occurrence of sorted sets.

In order to estimate storage requirements and to calculate the number of page accesses per operation, the page size and the maximum, minimum, and average record size are the remaining static parameters required.

As for dynamic parameters, the data base of an organization is ordinarily used and manipulated in a different manner by the various applications or transactions. It may be possible, however, to broadly categorize these transactions into a manageable number of classes. Furthermore, each class of transactions may be weighted according to its importance, that is, the percentage of all transactions that it represents.

Transactions may be classified on the basis of the operations that they perform and the frequency of such operations. Because it is possible to compare the performance of a DBC against that of a conventional computer in carrying out individual operations, it is therefore also possible to estimate the performance of a DBC on each class of transactions.

A number of measurements is suggested for the analysis (and classification) of transactions. Each operation, such as a sequential scan of records in any area, requires accesses to the data base storage. The number of accesses needed for an operation can be determined from a knowledge of the static parameters of the data base. The comparative performance of the DBC in the execution of individual (classes of) transactions can thereby be determined.

The following measurements are needed in connection with the retrieval of one or more records from the data base:

1. Total number of sequential scans of records in an area, irrespective of record type. This operation may be quite uncommon and may be done for reorganization of areas, for instance. The operation is performed procedurally, that is, a single record at a time.

2. Total number sequential scans of a specific type of record in an area. This operation may be necessary in order to find all occurrences of a record type that satisfy a certain condition. The operation is performed procedurally.

3. Total number of retrievals of a specific record occurrence (and/or its duplicates, in case the location mode is CALC) of a specific record type.
   a. When given a data base key and the location made is DIRECT.
   b. When given a CALC key and the location mode is CALC. This operation corresponds to the format 1 and format 5 FIND statements of the DML (of the April 1971 report),[4] followed by a GET.

4. Total number of traversals (performed procedurally or by the system) of an entire set occurrence when:
   a. The set is clustered.
   b. The set is not clustered. This operation is perhaps the most common of all record retrieval operations. The operation is often performed procedurally, one record at a time, and sometimes by the system, such as in response to a format 6 FIND statement. (A format 6 FIND statement requires that a record be found in a set occurrence that satisfies a given condition. Furthermore, the set occurrence itself

may have to be automatically selected and may sometimes require the traversal of other sets.)[5]

Finally, the storage (deletion) of records into (from) the data base, insertion (removal) of records into (from) sets, and modification of records are data manipulation operations. Measurements for these dynamic parameters are needed as follows:

1. Average number of clustered set occurrences procedurally traversed or traversed by the system to:
    a. Insert a record in a set occurrence.
    b. Remove a record from a set occurence.
    c. Store a record.
    d. Delete a record.
    e) Modify a record.
2. Average number of unclustered set occurrences procedurally traversed or traversed by the system to:
    a. Insert a record in a set occurrence.
    b. Remove a record from a set occurrence.
    c. Store a record in the data base.
    d. Delete a record from the data base.
    e. Modify a record.
3. Total number of times an operation takes place in which a record is
    a. Inserted.
    b. Removed.
    c. Stored.
    d. Deleted.
    e. Modified.

Application Development

Application development performance can be considered in a similar manner to operational performance. A data processing department has a certain application development throughput and response time. How many applications can the department develop in a given period of time and how long does it take from the time the application is requested until it is operational? Also, as systems become easier to use, applications will be developed by groups that are not actually involved in data processing. The time these people spend also must be measured. Because application development performance also depends on the complexity of the applications, the same set of benchmark applications previously described is used.

Because of rapdily increasing personnel costs, as much as possible should be done to reduce both the application development and the software maintenance time, effort, and cost. Estimating the magnitude of these tasks and evaluating them in light of particular data base computer system architectures will aid in evaluating these architectures.

This section has three parts corresponding to the three basic criteria. The most important one is ease of use. The other two more specialized criteria are backup and recovery and conversion.

Ease of use. Ease of use involves how much the user has to know about the data base, that is, the way the data is structured and organized, and about the DBMS. There are three types of users to consider: the data base administrator, the programming user, and the nonprogramming end user. The data base administrator (DBA) must know far more about both the data base and the DBMS than the applications programmer, who in turn must know more than the nonprogramming end user. Determining how easy a system is to use is very important, since productivity is directly related to ease of use. New personnel can be trained in less time and at lower training costs. In addition, many tasks can be assumed by less-skilled, lower-paid personnel. For example, with a high-level query language, many queries can be done by clerical rather than programming personnel.

CODASYL or network data systems are not very easy to use. The user must know all the record types, what data they contain, and how to access them. Because navigation through the data structure is required, one must keep track of his current position within each record type and set. Although there are high-level languages such as QLP#1100 which do much of this work for the user, the system architecture is not really compatible with these types of high-level operations.[6]

Although frequently overlooked, ease of use is also important for the data base administrator. The DBA estimates (with the users' help) the data needed in the data base and how it is going to be used. Then the DBA must develop a good data base design, based on these frequently inaccurate usage estimates. Any mistake in access methods, pointer definition, or set ordering can seriously degrade the system performance. Therefore, the less information the DBA must specify about the data base structure, the easier it is for him to design the data base and the less critical will be the user estimates.

One way to quantify ease of use is to determine what types of information and how much of each type is needed to develop an application. For example, does the user have to know how to access a particular record type or can he simply ask for all records of that type which satisfy a given selection expression? Therefore, to evaluate ease of use, the amount of information required by each type of user must be identified. A DBC architecture should rank higher with respect to ease of use if it requires less information.

Backup and Recovery. Backup and recovery are also related to application development through ease of use. The user should not have to initiate any explicit protection actions, aside from indicating the degree of protection required. The DBC architecture should be compatible with automatic backup and recovery procedures. This is particularly important because the DBC's high-level facilities will allow less skilled and knowledgeable users to access the data base. In any case, a user should not be able to change the data base or affect another user in such a way as to prevent restoration of the previous state if desired. The DBC architectures should be evaluated, then, to determine how well these backup and recovery criteria are met.

Conversion. Because most DBC architectures have a relational orientation, while very few current data bases are relational, either conversion or redesign is required. Conversion of the data base is preferable to redesign and should be minimized. It appears that limiting the conversion to a single essentially automatic conversion of the data base is possible.[7] This would involve replacing pointer-based access paths with content-based paths, for example eliminating owner-member set pointers by placing the set defining data items in both the owner and member record types. This approach is highly desirable since it does not require any labor-intensive program conversion. Although system performance will improve if low-level, record-at-a-time navigation-oriented queries and applications are changed to high-level, set-oriented operations, this type of application redesign becomes an option which the user may or may not select. Thus evaluation involves determining how much conversion is required by each architecture and the performance differences between the converted and redesigned system.

4-2. Cost

The decision to incorporate a data base computer into one's data processing system and then which DBC to select is usually made by weighing the cost considerations against the benefits, both real and potential. The cost factors include one-time as well as recurring costs.

Prime among the one-time costs is the purchase cost. In addition to the purchase price, the interest rate for borrowing this money must be taken into account. Another factor at work here is the "opportunity cost" to the purchaser.[8] Would this money be better spent on other computers or computer components? An example would be additional large-scale processors that could improve the communications handling capabilities or execute more application programs per time interval instead of or in addition to improvement in the data management area. Another possibility is that the money could be used in other non-data-processing-related operations of the company.

Competitive data base computer systems may influence the price that the manufacturer can charge. To date, only one special-purpose commercial product in this area has been "announced."[9] Most of the proposed data base computer designs, however, use existing technology, and it may be possible to reasonably estimate their costs. In the long run, though, prices could vary significantly depending on the features offered. In general, competitive pressures and advances in technology will serve to reduce the costs of data base computers and therefore will influence the purchase decision.

Other one-time costs are installation, testing, and conversion costs. Because most data base computer designs would fit into a standard single cabinet if implemented, installation costs should be minimal. Conversion costs to the user must be reasonable, or these systems will not be sold. Manufacturers will have to supply automated data base conversion aids for existing data bases. In addition, current data base application programs must still be supported. Any changes to these programs should be transparent to the user. Testing should be relatively straightforward for existing applications. With the new functionality that may be provided, for example, natural language query capabilities or relational data base systems, more extensive testing may be required.

If the DBC is rented instead of purchased, these rental costs must be placed under recurring costs. Other repetitive costs include maintenance, operation, and costs incurred while the DBC system is inoperative.

Another major recurring cost item is programming costs. Changes to existing programs now operating in a data base computer system environment as well as programs for new applications must be considered.

The key to the costs of a data base computer system involve basic trade-offs between hardware and software costs, with software further divided into system and application software. From another perspective, the difference between system and application software corresponds to the manufacturer's and user's viewpoints. Hardware and system software can be made less expensive (from the manufacturer's perspective) if many supporting functions are left for the user's application software. There is a contradiction here involving the ease-of-use criterion. The hardware cost trends suggest that, where possible, a function should be moved from the application into the hardware. This will reduce the recurring software costs and make the data base computer system more attractive to the user.

The benefits of a data base computer, as discussed in chapter 1, include increased performance and additional functionality. How much one should pay for these depends on the user's data base management requirements. Data base computers may not be cost-effective for every computer system.

It has been estimated that for those installations whose data management activity is less than 20 percent, a data base computer may not be necessary.[10] Thus acquiring a data base computer is a result of deciding that the benefits obtained justify the (life-cycle) costs. With the trends to more complex queries, more users of a data base, and larger data bases in general, it should be easier to justify installing a special-purpose computer for data base processing.

4-3. Range

The range criteria are measures of the variety of capability and capacity options provided by a DBC architecture. Given two otherwise comparable architectures, the one with the greater range of options can be tailored to the requirements of a wider variety of users. Nine basic factors are considered in this section.

Functional Capabilities

Different DBC configurations may support different sets of functions. Chapter 2 identified a relatively complete set of functional requirements. While a large-scale DBC would support all these functions, an entry-level DBC might provide only the basic functions. Similarly, a DBC and its associated software might support a single data model, while a more sophisticated version might support several different models, for example network and relational. This would allow the purchaser of a DBC to identify the functions needed and to select a DBC configuration with this capability. As requirements change or as data base technology evolves, it should be possible to add new functions to the system without drastic changes. Therefore, various architectures should be evaluated according to the range of functions provided and the ease with which new functions can be added.

Modularity

The modularity criterion refers to the internal architecture of the DBC. If the interfaces between the various components, for example, processing elements, memory, and mass storage devices, are well defined, then additional components might be easily added to the system. This modularity is useful for a number of reasons. First, by adding more modules of the elements that are involved in a bottleneck situation, the performance of the DBC can be improved. This would offer one means for expansion for the user with an increased data base load. Second, if additional elements can be easily added, various levels of reliability can be built into the system by providing spare or redundant elements. Therefore, an evaluation should be made as to the degree of modularity provided by a particular data base computer system architecture.

DBC Family

A family of DBCs is another means to upgrade a system as the data base workload increases. One way to implement a family of DBCs is to use the type of modular architecture described earlier. The important factor for this criterion, however, is that there be a series of specific systems whose external architecture appears the same. In practice, the user does not have to be aware of the differences in internal architectures. Obviously, from a manufacturer's viewpoint, the greater the commonality in the members of the family the better. The user has a ready migration path once he has committed himself to the DBC approach. A data base computer system should be rated on its inclusion or its potential for inclusion in a family of data base computer systems.

Host Dependencies

In most cases, the DBC will be directly attached to a host. Therefore, certain characteristics of acceptable host systems provide useful DBC evaluation criteria. At one end of the scale are those DBCs which can be connected only to a single type of host. In the middle are those which are compatible with an entire family of hosts, for example, 1100s or 370s. At the other end are those compatible with heterogeneous computers. Because the members of the host family vary in terms of costs and performance, ideally the same should apply to the DBC. An entry-level DBC would be used with either a small or large host, whereas a large-scale DBC would probably be attached only to a large-scale host. The possibility does exist, however, for those installations which are almost completely involved with data base management activities to install a large DBC and reduce the size of the present host.

A second factor to be considered is the compatibility of the DBC with several host families. The higher the level of the interface between the DBC and the host, the simpler this will be. Any parts of the DBC architecture which would limit its compatibility with different host families could be a serious handicap. Therefore, these various compatibility factors should be noted in the data base computer evaluation process.

View Support

Another range criterion is the number of data models the DBC can support. The relational data model seems to offer the best performance through taking advantage of the processing parallelism offered by the variety of DBC architectures. There are currently, however, few users with relational data bases. Most data bases are network or hierarchical (a restricted case of a network). Therefore, for efficiency, the DBC might support the relational data model, while for compatibility, it might support a network structure. The common data model now being studied provides one vehicle for supporting these views.[11] Therefore, data base computers should be evaluated on the number of views and which views they support.

A related question is whether the DBC also should support conventional file systems. For this type of file processing, most of the DBC architectures offer few performance benefits. For sequential file processing and for randomly retrieving specific records given a key value, conventional architectures appear adequate. Therefore, it is probably only a minor benefit if the architecture also supports conventional file systems. If the DBC architecture provided significant improvements for certain tasks such as sorting, however, current file system operation could be improved. For the DBC to be able to do this, the user would have to provide a minimal data definition for his files. Ideally, the DBC would have a very complete data definition for the data base. If it were going to support file systems as well, however, then it should also be able to operate with a minimal data definition of the files. Operating in this way, a DBC could provide an intermediate step in progressing from file systems to data base systems that would ease the user's move. The possibility of supporting current file systems and the benefits gained thereby should also form a part of the data base computer evaluation.

Multiple DBC Configurations

DBCs have two potential limits: processing power and storage. Expansions in processing power have been considered previously under subsections "Modularity" and "DBC Family." Another possible alternative is to use multiple DBCs. However, this approach has a basic constraint. Because the DBC provides the central point of control for data base integrity and security, a data base cannot be split across DBCs. If an installation were to have two independent data bases that were too large for a single DBC, then it would be possible to use two DBCs, each with its own data base.

There is another way in which multiple DBCs could share a data base. If all the operations requiring locks on the data base were always routed to one of the DBCs and if the other DBC were used only for retrieval, the integrity of the data base would remain protected. Certain queries would result in invalid results, however, if the other DBC were in the middle of updating the requested data. Multiple DBC configurations of this type, therefore, remain a topic for further research, and this evaluation criterion may have to be held in abeyance until these multiple configuration problems are solved.

A multiple DBC configuration is, however, more viable as an approach to reliability. Modularity can provide increased reliability by allowing spare elements to be built into the system. At another level, multiple DBCs also could be used in this manner for improved reliability. In the preceding example there may be two DBCs, each controlling one of a center's two data bases. When one of the DBCs fails, the other one could take over and control both the data bases (although with degraded performance for each). The ability to configure DBCs in this manner should be considered in the evaluation.

Distributed Processing Configurations

Because distributed processing and distributed data bases are rapidly growing areas, a DBC architecture also should be applicable to this environment. The simplest approach is to attach the DBC's host to the network and perform all the communications processing on either the host or its communications front-end. In certain cases, for example, the DATACOMPUTER on ARPANET,[12] it may be desirable to attach a stand-alone DBC directly to a network. This requires that the DBC either perform the communications functions or have a direct interface to a communications front-end. A modular approach here (see subsection "Modularity") would allow for the addition of a communication module for just this type of situation. Also, if the DBC architecture allows it to connect to several different host families (see subsection "Host Dependencies"), it would be easier to use in a distributed environment. Therefore, this criterion should evaluate how easily an architecture can be integrated into a distributed environment and how diverse this environment can be with respect to the number of nodes and variety of hosts that can be supported.

Range of Applications

A DBC architecture may exhibit very different performances for different types of applications. Examples of these types include retrieval of a single record or a set of records based on a single key value or a complex selection expression, searching ordered or unordered sets, searching clustered or unclustered sets, sorting, and high or low update volumes. The broader the range of applications for which an architecture is effective, the greater the potential uses for that architecture. Therefore, this criterion concerns the distribution of performance across a range of applications. The best way to measure this criterion is to determine a weighted performance based on the frequency or importance of each type of application type.

Fault Tolerance

Fault tolerance is another important factor in evaluating data base computers. Because the only path from the host to the data is through the DBC, tolerance to faults is critical. If the DBC fails, the data base is unavailable, even though it may not be damaged. For this reason, the DBC architecture must allow for graceful degradation and avoid catastrophic failure. On the other hand, while this capability is important, it is not free. It may increase hardware costs and system software complexity while reducing performance, that is, throughput and response time.

Factors to increase fault tolerance can occur at several levels. Internal to the DBC, the use of highly reliable components, error-correcting codes, and automatic instruction retry all improve the fault-tolerance characteristics of the system. A modular design will also increase an architecture's fault tolerance. Modularity refers to the internal architecture of the DBC. If the interface between the various components, that is, processing elements, memory, and disk tracks, is clean and well-defined, then additional components can be easily added to the system. This type of architecture allows various levels of reliability to be built into the system by providing spare or redundant elements. Architectures with the more modular design, therefore, appear to be more desirable.

When there is a failure in the DBC, there are two additional ways to increase the overall fault tolerance of the system. The most general approach would be to allow multiple DBCs (see subsection "Multiple DBC Configurations") so that when one fails the others can continue processing, although in a degraded mode. A more restricted approach would be to shift some of the DBC functions to the host. This approach does have a number of potential problems, but it should be considered.

The fault-tolerance criterion should be used to determine that an acceptable range of fault-tolerance alternatives for the data base computer system is available. The choice of a particular set of fault-tolerant techniques from these alternatives can then be made by the user based on cost, performance, and other criteria.

4-4. Evolvability

This set of criteria involves the way in which the DBC can adjust to changes in technologies or data base size and activity. It is used to evaluate the useful life of a data base computer.

New Technologies

If the DBC architecture is relatively modular with clean well–defined interfaces between its components, individual components can be upgraded and replaced as the appropriate new technologies emerge. For example, bubble or charge–coupled storage devices (when they become available in production quantities) might replace existing storage devices with little or no modification of the DBC's basic architecture. Measuring this criterion requires a determination of the number and type of components of a particular architecture that have the necessary clean interfaces in order to incorporate new technologies in the system.

Data Base Size

The basic trend is to larger and larger data bases. One applications analysis found an average data base size of 600 megabytes.[13] The Social Security Administration is designing a data base with over 90 billion bytes on–line and another 370 billion bytes in off–line and archival storage. Although very large data bases like this are currently the exception, they are representative of the trend. This means that while the DBC does not have to be able to handle data bases this large at present, the architecture should have the potential to grow to handle these very large sizes.

This growth potential has two requirements. First, the data base computer architecture should be expandable to store and access these very large data volumes. Second, the architecture also should allow a corresponding increase in the parallelism without which these increased volumes would result in prohibitive response times.

Measuring these criteria simply involves ranking the various data base computers in terms of the size data base they can support and the amount of parallelism they support and determining how much the size and parallelism can be increased before significant changes in the architecture are required.

Summary

A large number of items were established in this chapter as the basis for evaluating data base computers and possible system configurations. Each of the criteria was defined and its value explained. In general, an individual item is not an absolute measure but instead has to be considered and evaluated in conjunction with all the others. Also included in this chapter were proposals to determine or measure the various factors through analyses, benchmarks, and simulations.

The evaluation criteria were divided into four categories: performance, cost, range, and evolvability. The performance area covered both operational and application development. The operational criteria apply to the system performance, in terms of throughput, response time, and backup and recovery measures, for a particular application or mix of applications. The application development criteria apply to the complexity, in terms of ease of use, conversion, and backup and recovery, involved in developing an application that will execute on a system incorporating a data base computer.

Throughput and response time are relatively straightforward operational performance measures. Throughput is a count of the number of transactions or jobs that can be processed in a given period of time, while response time is the interval between entering the last character of a message and receiving the first character of the response. Backup and recovery, however, are more complex. First, the period of time that the data base or portions thereof are unavailable following a failure or error must be determined. Second, the overhead associated with each transaction in support of the backup and recovery procedures must be found.

Benchmarking and simulation were two methods proposed to evaluate the data base computer system performance. First, performance measurements for a network data base benchmark executing under a data management system should be obtained. Next, using the same data base activity profile, performance measures for the various data base computer systems must be estimated. For this, both the selected network data base and its equivalent relational version are needed. Then, through simulations using perhaps a network queuing model approach, the estimated performance can be obtained.

Application development performance was considered in a similar manner to operational performance. Because this performance also depends on the complexity of the applications, the same set of benchmarks as for operational performance can be used. The items in this area, however, are related to personnel activities and therefore are more difficult to quantify and analyze.

Determining and evaluating the costs of a data base computer system should be made in relation to the benefits to be obtained. Costs estimates must be made for both one-time and recurring costs. Also, consideration must be given to the basic hardware–software tradeoffs that would affect items in each of these cost categories.

The measure of the variety of capability and capacity options provided by the data base computer is included in the range category. Different options allow the basic DBC architecture to be tailored to the requirements of a variety of users. One type of proposed evaluation is on the basis of scope of functionality provided and the ease with which new functionality can be added. Other criteria include degree of modularity offered, potential for expansion into a family of data base computer systems, and compatibility with various hosts and host families.

Configurations of data base computers also fall into the range evaluation criteria. The ability to configure multiple data base computers to increase processing power, allow larger data bases, and/or provide more tolerance to faults should be determined and rated. The DBC also should be considered in light of the growing trend toward distributed systems.

A final set of range criteria is related to user applications. Optimization for a particular type as opposed to a wide range of applications should be determined. Support of multiple views (network, relational, and so on), and which ones, needs to be evaluated. Finally, the possibility of supporting current file system applications and the benefits gained thereby form a part of the data base computer evaluation.

The final evaluation category, evolvability, applies to the period of usefulness of a data base computer. It is a measure of the adaptability of the DBC to changes in technologies or data base size and activity. Identifying the number and type of DBC components that have clean, well–defined interfaces can be used in assessing the potential for incorporating new technologies. Determining the data base size and amount of parallelism supportable and the degree that these items can be increased before significant changes in the architecture are required is used to evaluate the effects of changing data base size and activity.

Notes

1. O.H. Bray and H.A. Freeman, "Data Usage and the Data Base Processor," *Proceedings of the ACM '78*, December 1978, pp. 234–240.

2. G.S. Graham, "Queuing Network Models of Computer System Performance," *Computing Surveys* 10, No. 3, September 1978, pp. 219–224.

3. *Conference of Data Systems Languages (CODASYL) Data Base Task Group Report,* ACM, New York, April 1971.

4. Ibid.

5. Ibid.

6. Sperry Univac, *Query Language Processor (QLP 1100)*, UP–8231 Rev. 1, 1977.

7. H.R. Johnson and J.A. Larson, "Data Management for Microcomputers," *Proceedings Compcon '79 Fall,* September 1979.

8. G.A. Champine, "Univac's Financial Model for Computer Development," *Datamation,* February 1977, pp. 53–57.

9. J. Verity, "Data Base Growth Spurs Back-End Unit Evolution," *Electronic News,* March 20, 1978, p. 36.

10. G.A. Champine, "Four Approaches to a Data Base Computer," *Datamation,* December 1978, pp. 101–106.

11. Johnson et al., "Data Management for Microcomputers."

12. T. Marill and D. Stern, "The Datacomputer—A Network Data Utility," *AFIPS Conference Proceedings* 44, 1975 NCC, June 1975, pp. 388–395.

13. Bray and Freeman, "Data Usage."

5 Data Base Computer Architectures

The first section in this chapter describes a data base computer classification scheme and discusses the significant advantages and disadvantages of each category. The taxonomy involves two dimensions: one based on where the data base is searched, and the other on the number of processors involved. The search may be performed directly on the device where the data base is permanently stored, or a part of the data base may be staged to some intermediate storage device and searched there. The latter approach is classified as an indirect search of the data base. The second dimension involves the number of processors performing the search. The important distinction is whether or not there is parallel processing, not the actual number of processors being used, because as long as more than one processor is involved, certain interface and coordination problems arise.

The next five sections, each of which has the same basic organization, consider each of the architectural approaches in more detail. First, there is a general description of the architecture and a more detailed explanation of its advantages and disadvantages. Second, there is a description of an actual system or design using the architecture. Third, there is a description of how the example data base and the typical queries established in chapter 3 would be handled on the system.

The first of the five systems that are described is the conventional general–purpose processor used as a back–end, an example of the single processor indirect search approach. The second approach is illustrated with the ICL CAFS system.[1] Although this system uses a special–purpose processor, it involves only a single processor, thereby avoiding the coordination problems normally associated with parallel processing. Although the search in this system is not really direct in the sense that it actually takes place at the storage device, it is a major step in this direction. In fact, it is as close to a direct search as possible with any single–processor architecture. In this case, the data are searched as they are read, with only the selected data actually moved further into the system. The next approach, a direct search by multiple processors, is used by CASSM.[2] STARAN[3] and RAP[4] involve multiple processors doing an indiresct search of that part of the data base which has been staged into a faster intermediate or associative storage. Finally, the DBC[5] developed at Ohio State is described as a combined system which uses parallel processors to directly search a part of the data base. Before returning the selected part of the data base to the host, however, DBC may do some additional indirect searching and processing.

5-1. Categorization

As an aid in evaluating a data base computer for a particular environment and in comparing the various designs, a classification of the types of special-purpose computers is required. Several schemes have already been proposed based on their generic descriptions as "back-end" machines. Rosenthal has identified three distinct classes of these types of data management devices:

1. Large host back-end.
2. Distributed network data node.
3. Smart peripheral.

The classification is based on the number of functions off-loaded from the host to the back-end data base machine. The large host back-end is placed between the host and the data base, has exclusive access to the data, and performs arious data base management services for the host. The network data machine provides the same type of service for several hosts in a network rather than to just a specific host. The smart peripheral designation associates data management hardware and functions with mass storage device controllers. The special-purpose approaches of CASSM and RAP are lumped together in this third category. Although this categorization describes possible functions of a data base machine in a computing system, it reveals nothing about the architecture or characteristics of such devices. Given a different complement of software, a particular data base computer could be placed in another category.

A recent proposal by Banerjee, Baum, and Hsiao of a classification that distinguishes various designs is somewhat of an improvement.[7] In addition to the category of back-end machine, they have one for high-speed processors and another for logic-per-track approaches. The high-speed processor approach involves staging data from mass storage into a high-speed parallel processing device. An example of this classification would be RAP. The logic-per-track approach involves associating processing logic with some or all tracks of a disk or other rotating storage device, as in CASSM. Hsiao's own DBC is discussed as a combination back-end machine and logic-per-track device. The problem with their categorization is that architecture (logic-per-track), function (back-end), and performance (high speed) are not mutually exclusive.

To avoid the problems of these previously described categories, a new classification, based on hardware architecture, has been developed. The two criteria established for this classification scheme are the number of processing elements involved in the data base processing and the type of hardware organization used to search for the data directly on mass storage devices or indirectly in some buffered or intermediate storage area. The five categories comprising this classification scheme are

1. Single processor indirect search (SPIS).
2. Single processor direct search (SPDS).
3. Multiple processor direct search (MPDS).
4. Multiple processor indirect search (MPIS).
5. Multiple processor combined search (MPCS).

The number of parallel processing elements used is important because it directly relates to performance. The types of requests that typically occur in a data base management operation involving the search of an entire file or data base lend themselves very well to parallel processing. In these cases, if the file or data base were divided into blocks of data, a set of parallel processing elements could perform the search much faster than a single processing element. In addition, with the cost of hardware dropping by a factor of 20 to 30 percent a year, microprocessors, LSI, or VLSI devices are a very cost-effective means of implementing parallel processing. Almost all the proposed data base computer designs that show or claim significant performance improvement (CASSM, RAP, DBC, STARAN, and so on) employ parallel processing logic. In fact, the general-purpose computer used as a back-end and ICL's CAFS are the only exceptions to the use of parallel processing, and even CAFS appears to have a limited parallel processing capability.

Where the data base is searched also affects performance. The search may be performed directly on the mass storage unit where the data base is permanently stored or indirectly in some intermediate storage area. The objective is to perform the search as close to the source as possible to avoid the delays inherent in unnecessary data movement. Because of the rotational and transfer speeds of mass storage devices today, however, most of the direct searches can involve only very simple selections. Complex Boolean expressions just cannot be evaluated without skipping records, requiring one or more disk revolutions. The result is that there is a tradeoff involved between query complexity and performance, and the choice between a direct-search data base computer and an indirect one may depend on the applications involved. One design, Hsiao's DBC (described in section 5-6), handles this issue by directly searching the data with track processors for simple queries and staging the data in buffers in the DBC for more complex evaluations.

5-2. Single Processor Indirect Search

The single processor indirect search (SPIS) corresponds to the conventional general-purpose processor. In this traditional approach, part of the data base is read from its permanent storage on moving head disks into the intermediate staging storage of random access memory. Index tables and pointers are used to determine which part or parts of the data base are staged into the system's main memory. This block of data is then processed to determine the records that are to be retrieved or modified. Although the implementation details may differ, all current DBMSs operate essentially in this manner. For example, with an indexed sequential access method, the part of the data base that is to be loaded is selected by the primary key values. In a CODASYL data base, members of a set are frequently stored near their owner records so that obtaining a single block of data increases the likelihood that all the desired records will be found when the block is searched.

The last three sections of chapter 3 described in considerable detail how this type of architecture would process the typical transactions against the example data base. The main difference is that chapter 3 described a system in which both the applications and the DBMS executed in the same machine, whereas with a general-purpose back-end data base computer, they would reside and execute in different machines. Separate computers are obviously inefficient for low-level, record-at-a-time requests because a request message would have to be passed from the host to the data base computer to locate the record and then another message, the selected record, would have to be passed from the data base computer to the host. Even though the data management activity is off-loaded from the host in this case, there is the added overhead associated with the two messages transferred between the host and the data base computer for every record retrieved. For record-at-a-time operations, therefore, this approach could actually degrade the system's performance. On the other hand, this is not true for high-level queries because the data base computer can relieve the host of a significant amount of work between the time it receives a request and the time it returns a response, which may include many records. This potential performance improvement was recognized by the Computer Corporation of America (CCA) very early in the Datacomputer project when a high-level query language for ARPANET users of the Data-computer was defined and implemented.[8]

5-3. Single Processor Direct Search

Approach

The single processor direct search (SPDS) approach, as well as all the others that will be described in this chapter, involve some type of special-purpose hardware to more effectively implement the data base management function. In this approach, the data are searched by the special-purpose device, with the result that only the desired records or their specified parts need to be sent to the host. This reduction in data volume, through selection and projection operations, significantly reduces the load on the host by eliminating many relatively simple tests on large masses of data that were normally performed by the host. In fact, the software just to read the data into the host is much more complex and time consuming than that required for the tests to determine if the data are of interest.

In conventional systems, the data flow simultaneously from several devices through multiple I/O channels to the host. In the SPDS approach, specially designed hardware is placed between the channels and the host. There could be a separate device for each channel or the channels could be multiplexed through a single element with sufficiently fast data base computer hardware.

This approach is classified as a direct search because intermediate storage is not used for the data search even though these data are not actually directly searched on the storage device. By not having this intermediate storage, however, only a limited set of search–type operations and not a complete data base management system can be supported. DBMS functions such as security, integrity checking, locking, and data conversion must still be performed in the host. Also, the host decides which blocks of data are read to find the desired records. Although this type of data base computer has its shortcomings, the advantage is that a host–initiated read of a thousand records may result in 99 percent of them being eliminated by the data base computer. The host, then, would have to handle only the remaining 1 percent.

ICL CAFS Architecture

CAFS (Content Addressable File Store) was designed by ICL as a high-speed search device and is an example of the single processor direct search approach.[9] Because CAFS does not use the additional definition information provided in the data base schema, it can be used to process file as well as data base systems.

Figure 5-1 shows the overall architecture of a system which includes CAFS. The data base and files are stored on conventional disks which read one track at a time or on parallel disks which read half the tracks on a cylinder in a single revolution. To obtain an even higher data rate, the outputs from several disks, of either or both types, can be multiplexed. Data from the disks flow through a minicomputer-controlled pipeline where the selection is performed. Records which meet the selection criteria are then passed on to the host. When CAFS is used to support file systems, the records are finally presented to the user and the processing is complete. If a DBMS is involved, however, all the DBMS functions other than selection are performed by the DBMS on the host computer before the data are finally sent to the user.

CAFS allows fixed- or variable-length records and fixed- or variable-

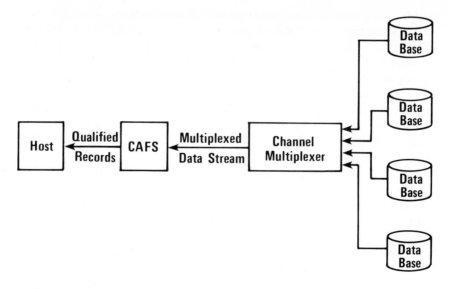

Figure 5-1. CAFS—Incorporated Retrieval System.

length fields within these records. Rather than a single template for all the records of a particular type, each field within the record is labeled and contains a length code.

Figure 5-2 shows the major components comprising the internal architecture of CAFS. Sixteen key registers are used in the comparisons as the data are streamed through the system. First, the keyword variable name and a value are loaded into the key register. Then, as a record is read, it is processed simultaneously by each key register. The label fields in each record ensure that the value in the key register is compared only to the appropriate field within the record; that is, when the label fields match, then the values are compared. The results of these comparisons determine which one of the three gates to set: a less than, an equal, and a greater than gate. These results also are passed to the search–evaluation unit to evaluate the complete logical expression of the query. Multiple 64K bit array stores are incorporated in CAFS for joins and the elimination of duplicates following projections and may be used to hold input data for the search–evaluation unit. Finally, there is a retrieval unit to hold the record in its buffer until a determination of the record's qualification is made. If the record is qualified, the search–evaluation unit sets a switch which allows the record to be passed to the host. If not, the record is replaced or overwritten when the next record is read into the retrieval unit.

The essential problem that CAFS addressed was the rapid location and

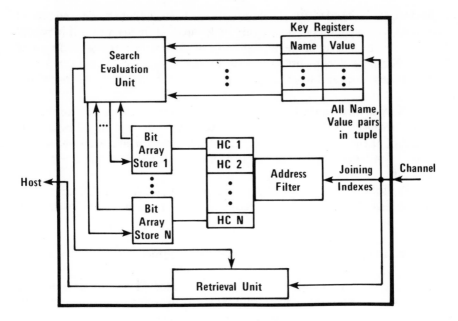

Figure 5–2. CAFS Architecture.

retrieval of records when the selection criteria are based on data values within the record rather than the record's position. There is just too much processing and storage overhead to use conventional pointers and indexes to specific records in this task. The problem is even more severe when many or all of the fields in the record can be used as search keys. Also, scanning very large files is simply too time consuming, even with a high–speed search device. CAFS was designed to overcome these problems through the use of coarse pointers to large blocks of data, for example, a track, rather than individual records. This block is then scanned to locate the desired records. Also, hashing methods can be used in addition to or instead of pointers if the data are ultimately to be located with a scan. Furthermore, any occurrence of synonyms is resolved during the scan.

CAFS was also an attempt to solve the partial key problem, where only a part of the key on which the data are indexed is known. Directory assistance is an example of one application where this type of problem regularly occurs. For example, find the telephone number of the Thompson who lives somewhere on Main Street. Moreover, the name actually may be spelled Thomson. With most conventional indexing methods, such a query is extremely difficult, if not impossible, to process. If part of the retrieval were to involve a scan of the records, however, only the known part of the field would be needed for the comparison. Then, either the desired record or a set which contains it can easily be located. In many ways, this partial key problem is closer to the information or document retrieval problem of libraries where documents are to be located based on the occurrence of certain keywords and where all the possible keywords cannot be specified a priori.

Many of the transactions described in chapter 3 cannot be applied to CAFS because it is strictly a retrieval system and thus does not allow on-line updating of the data. In addition, CAFS searches for and retrieves sets of records but leaves the higher-level functions, such as sum and average, to the host.

The following illustrates CAFS's processing of several different types of queries. The last example explains the use of the bit store in the join operation.

List all the order numbers and dates for customer *ABC*.

For this query, the order relation is first located on the mass storage device and a read of that device is initiated. At the same time, one of the key registers is loaded with the appropriate key and value pair. In this particular example, the key is customer number and the value is *ABC*. As the order records are streamed through CAFS, each field label is checked to see if it is a customer number. When the customer number is encountered, it is compared to value *ABC*. The three gates are then set to the appropriate Boolean values, depending on whether the value in the record is less than, equal to, or greater than *ABC*. Because the other key registers are simultaneously testing other fields within the record, either several parts of a single query or many different queries can be processed concurrently for the same set of records.

The outputs of the three gates for each key register are passed to the search-evaluation unit, which performs the necessary logical operations to evaluate the selection expression. In this example, it simply examines the equals gate. If this gate is set, then the record qualifies as an answer to the query and a signal is sent to the retrieval unit to allow the record to be passed to the host.

List the order numbers for all the January orders for over $100 from customer *ABC*.

This more complex query could be processed at the same time as the previous one. In this case, three key registers are needed: one for the customer number, one for the month and one for the amount. If both queries were processed simultaneously, then only one key register would be needed for the customer number. If the two queries involved different customer numbers, then two key registers would be used because different keyword value pairs are involved.

As the records stream by the key registers, all the necessary comparisons are made and the appropriate gates are set. After each record is thus processed, the search-evaluation unit performs the necessary Boolean operations to combine the various keyword predicates. It also specifies which records should be sent from the retrieval unit to which user process on the host. In these two examples, the second query produces a subset of the responses to the first one, but the procedure is the same even if the queries result in nonoverlapping responses.

List the credit rating for all customers with an order valued over $1,000.

Using the converted data base, this query requires a join of the order and customer relations on the common field customer number. First, the order relation is located and searched to find all the orders with a value greater than $1,000. This is accomplished by loading the label value (order value) and the data value ($1,000) into a key register. The search-evaluation unit then checks for the greater than gate to be set. When it is, rather than sending the record to the host, the search-evaluation unit sets a bit in the bit array store. Next, the customer relation is processed. Each bit in the bit store corresponds to a potential customer number so that when each of these customer records is found, the identifier and the credit rating are sent to the host. This effectively implements the relational half join, that is, selection is performed on one relation and the common field is used to identify the corresponding tuples in the second relation from which the specified data are retrieved.

Two methods can be used for setting bits in the bit store as required for this query. The first uses a one-to-one correspondence between each bit (of the 64K bits in each bit store) and a specific value for the field that is used in a join operation. Then, when this value is encountered, the appropriate bit is set. To use this method, the domains common to the two relations must be specified a priori and a special joining index must be added to each relation. This joining index is simply an integer from 1 to N (64K) for each value of the join domain. The index value in the tuple corresponds to the value of the common domain.

In processing the order relation for this query, there is a joining index for customer number. This joining index is processed by the bit address filter and specifies which bit in the store to set. When the customer relation is processed, then its joining index for customer number results in the bit address filter generating a bit address. If the bit is set, then this customer record is selected and sent to the host. If not, then this customer would not have been found on the previous search, so this particular record would not qualify as an answer to the query.

Several conditions could prevent the use of this first method of setting the bit store. If the join were not anticipated when the data base was defined and created, then the joining index would not have been built. Also, if a concatenation of several domains as the basis for the join were desired, a combined index would probably not exist. Finally, if there are more unique values than there are bits in the bit store, it cannot be used. For these situations, the bits can be set and searched by a second method.

The second method of setting the bit store involves hashing in the determination of which bits to set. Independent hashing algorithms, shown in figure 5–2 as the HC units, are assigned to each of the several independent duplicate bit stores. When a qualified order record is read for this query, then the customer number is hashed using each of the several hashing functions. Each function specifies a bit in its corresponding bit store to be set. When the customer records are read, each customer number is also hashed using all the algorithms, and the proper bit in each store is checked. If all the bits are set to 1, it is assumed that this particular customer record is qualified.

The key word in the second approach is assumed. By using an arbitrary number of hashing functions and bits, the probability of an error can be made arbitrarily small but not zero. Also, because the error is caused by synonyms, the direction of the error is that too many records, not too few, are selected. For certain applications, such as directory assistance, this error is acceptable if its probability is small enough.

5–4. Multiple Processor Direct Search

Approach

Figure 5–3 illustrates the basic characteristics of the multiple processors direct search (MPDS) approach, of using a processor per track to directly search the data base. As the storage devices (for example, disks, magnetic bubbles, or charge couple devices) rotate, data are read into the corresponding track processor, which then examines the records to determine which ones should be selected or modified. Following a brief processing period, the data are written back to the same track as part of the same revolution. In effect, the data stream off the track, through the processor, and back to the same track. The amount of processing that can be performed on a single revolution, therefore, is limited by the speed of the processor and the speed of the rotating device. If processing is not completed in a single revolution, then flags are set in each record to indicate its selection and the degree of processing completed.

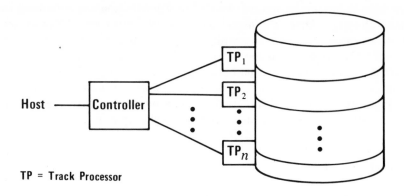

TP = Track Processor

Figure 5-3. Multiple Processor Direct Search.

With MPDS, the data volume through the system is reduced because the searches are done directly on the storage devices. Also, by having a head per track for the data base, the search time is essentially independent of the size of the data base, and the entire data base can be searched in a single revolution. In fact, with multiple compare registers, it may be possible to answer several requests in a single revolution. On the other hand, processing data on the fly can cause timing problems. For example, if a track processor cannot complete the examination of a record before the next one arrives, additional revolutions are required. In addition, other timing problems might arise if multiple records in a hierarchy or network must be examined to determine if a record in the structure is needed.

The tradeoff that has been made with the direct-search approach is to minimize the response time rather than the storage costs. Because all the tracks of the data base are read and processed in parallel, the basic unit of response time is independent of the data base size and is simply a function of the time to read a single track. Operations that require multiple revolutions have multiple unit response times. The penalty for this "constant response time" is the cost of storage. Storage costs increase linearly with the amount of data being stored for direct-search storage devices just as with conventional disks. The slope in this case, though, is much steeper because the direct-search devices also require a processing element for each track. It may be possible to reduce this cost in the future because of rapidly advancing hardware technology. For example, processing logic can be directly incorporated into magnetic bubble memory storage devices at little or no additional cost.[10]

One of the serious problems facing those MPDS architectures which continuously read from and write to the data base on every revolution is backup and recovery. Constantly rewriting the data base significantly increases the number of errors from that of a conventional system using the same technology. Given a constant error rate of 1 error per N bits written, writing a thousand times as many bits means a thousand times more errors. Also, if an error occurs during a write operation, the track must be reconstructed from the log file. The option to issue a command to rewrite the buffer, as in more conventional systems, does not exist because the data are continuously streaming through the processing elements. In the extreme case, a buffer the size of the entire data base would be required.

CASSM Architecture

The CASSM (Context Addressable Segment Sequential Memory) system developed at the University of Florida was specifically designed for general-purpose nonnumeric applications such as data management, information retrieval, and document processing.[11] Within the data base context, CASSM allows parallel processing of the data base so that the time required to perform many of the data management functions is independent of the size of the data base. In addition, CASSM directly supports in hardware a high-level user view of the data base. Although the relational data model can be supported, the basic data model for which the system was designed is hierarchical so that the user sees his data as a hierarchy or a set of integrated sequential files.

The original research effort on CASSM resulted in the construction of a prototype of a single cell of the basic architecture. A fixed-head disk was the data base storage device, with each track representing a cell in the system. Algorithms were defined, coded, and then tested on this single-cell configuration. More recent research on CASSM has involved simulation studies of the multicell architecture.[12] The algorithms were extended to the multicell case by allowing records and files to span cells and by developing methods for passing data and control information between cells. The performance of the algorithms and various test applications was then measured through simulations of different multicell configurations.

Each cell in the basic CASSM system shown in figure 5-4 contains both storage and processors. Files that are handled in this system are partitioned, and parts are placed in each cell to allow parallel processing of this information. The size of the data base that can be stored in this manner is a function of both the number of cells and the storage capacity of each cell. The time to process a request against this data base is a function of the amount of storage in each cell. Because the CASSM cell processors function in lock-step to process the same instruction against their own data, the entire data base can be processed in one disk revolution. If the data base is larger than the storage capacity provided by all the CASSM cells, it must be partitioned

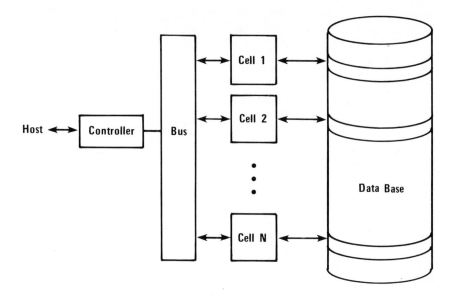

Figure 5-4. CASSM System Architecture.

and then staged into the available storage. Although this staging approach is one way to handle large data bases, CASSM was designed on the assumption that the entire data base can reside in the CASSM storage. While this allows the data base to be processed much faster than in a staged system such as STARAN, the cost per bit for storing this data base is much greater because additional storage and processors are needed as the data base grows.

As mentioned in the previous paragraphs, CASSM is a cellular architecture with each cell containing both storage and processing elements, as shown in figure 5-5. The storage can be implemented with fixed-head disks, magnetic bubbles, charge couple devices, or any other storage device whose technology is such that the data appear to be rotating past some fixed point. Then, as the data rotate, every word is read, processed, and written back to this storage device.

A CASSM word consists of 40 bits, 32 data bits, and 8 tag and status bits, formatted into one of the various words shown in figure 5-6. A three-bit tag field (figure 5-7) is used to identify the seven word types currently being used. These types include delimiter, data, pointer, instruction, operand, and others. First, the delimiter word indicates the beginning of a record. A code exists for the type of record or file which follows as well as its level in the data hierarchy. A six-bit stack indicates whether the record

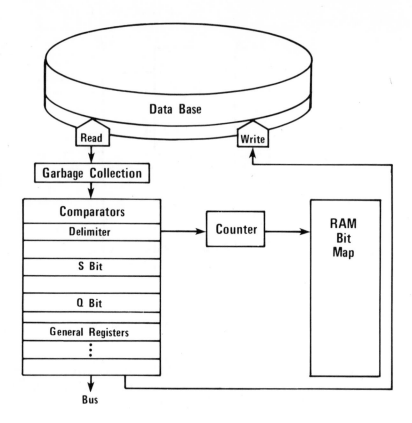

Figure 5-5. CASSM Cell Architecture.

meets certain search criteria. These stack bits are used in processing complex transactions requiring several revolutions to complete. For these types of transactions, the results for one revolution are saved in the stack bits while the remaining tests continue on the next revolution. In addition, a variety of Boolean operations can be performed on the bits in this stack and the match bits in each data word.

The next three types of formats are reserved for data and pointer words. Both the data and pointer words contain a name code and the actual data value. The name field is redundantly stored in each occurrence to provide greater flexibility by allowing variable-length records and repeating groups within a hierarchical data structure. This approach differs from the one taken by most of the relational-oriented systems, which require fixed-length and fixed-format records within each relation. In these other approaches, a single template is used to define the record format for any

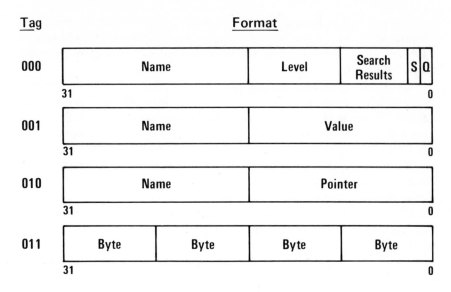

Figure 5–6. CASSM Data Word Formats.

Word Types	Tag Code	
Delimiter	000	
Name/Value	001	
Pointer	010	Data Words
String	011	
Instruction	100	
Stack/Queue	101	
Erase/Temp	111	

Figure 5–7. CASSM Word Types.

record type or relation. While this reduces the storage requirement by eliminating redundant names, it provides less flexibility for processing other data structures.

The fifth and sixth formats are used to identify instructions and their operands. An active bit indicates whether the instuction should be ignored or queued for execution. Setting the active bits in the appropriate instruction words is the CASSM equivalent of calling a subroutine.

The last format is used for one of several types of words depending on the three status bits. A temporary storage word, an end-of-file indicator, or a garbage word to be deleted by the automatic garbage-collection hardware may be indicated.

Unlike conventional rotating storage, a CASSM cell contains separate read and write heads. Every word of storage then can be read and, if it not deleted, written back on each revolution. Insertion or deletion is illustrated in figure 5-8 with an example of a five-word pipeline. First, a word is read from the storage device into the first word of the pipeline. As this occurs, each word in the pipeline is shifted down one position, with the fifth and last word shifted out of the pipeline and lost. For each word read and shifted into the pipeline, then, the write head must take one word and write it back to the storage device. Normally, the word in the middle of the pipeline (position 3) is written out. If that word is flagged as a garbage word to be deleted, however, the next word (currently in position 2) is selected and written out. For the rest of this revolution, all the words to be written out are selected from the second position. This procedure allows one garbage word to be removed from storage on each revolution. In this example, two words could be removed in a single revolution by performing the same operation again and writing out the remaining words from position 1.

The converse operation can be used to insert words in the data base. Instead of writing out the word in position 3, the word to be inserted is written out. The old word is not lost, though, because the output from the pipeline is shifted and selected from position 4. For the rest of the revolution, then, the words are written out from position 4 instead of the normal position 3. Also, just as two words could be deleted in this example, two words can be inserted on each revolution.

With a multicell configuration, deletion and insertion are slightly more complex. If a record spans two cells, deleting a word in the first cell moves all the remaining words in the record, including those in the following cell, by one position and requires a second revolution. To aid in this operation, there is a special register in each cell which holds the cell's first and last word. When a word in the first cell is deleted, the last word is moved up, and the contents of the first word register of the following cell is written out as the last word in the first cell. On the next revolution, then, this word which has been moved up, is deleted in the second cell. Similarly, when a word is inserted in the first cell, which then overflows into the second cell, the last word of the first cell is written out as the first word of the second cell on the second revolution.

The preceding techniques are appropriate when only a few words are to be inserted or deleted. For large blocks of data, special block inserts and deletes are possible. These operations move entire blocks of words from one cell to another cell to make room in the original cell for the data to be inserted or to fill in the gap left by a block of deleted data.

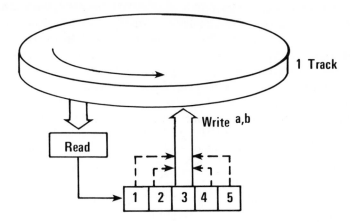

a. Normally from position 3, though, any position is possible
b. Small number of words

Figure 5-8. CASSM Insertion or Deletion.

CASSM was designed to be used in conjunction with a general-purpose processor. In normal operation, the user would issue a high-level data management command such as "List all the engineers in the production department." This command would then be translated into a set of instructions to be executed on CASSM. The result of this translation may be either the creation and loading of a set of CASSM instructions and operands or simply the loading of a set of operands and an activation of a set of data management primitives residing on the CASSM storage. In either case, the appropriate instructions are executed in parallel on each of the cells, and the responses are collected and returned to the user.

Instruction execution on CASSM occurs in three phases on different hardware in a pipeline architecture. In the first phase, the next instruction and its operands are located, fetched, and broadcast to all the cells during one revolution for execution in the second phase. During the second phase, all the cells execute the instruction against the entire data base. In the third or postexecution phase, the instruction is deactivated and its operands are deleted. While three revolutions are required to complete the execution of a single instruction, one instruction is executed, on the average, every revolution because three instructions execute concurrently. In addition, a number of support functions, such as automatic garbage collection, are performed concurrently with these search instructions. Words or records specified and marked for output are also collected and sent to the user during this time.

Although CASSM appears to offer significant improvement to data base management tasks, a number of deficiencies that restrict CASSM's applicability as a commercially viable data base computer are apparent. Perhaps some of these problems, such as too few data types and the restricted size of the data base, can be resolved. Other difficulties, such as the backup and recovery of a system with a continuous read and write cycle, may be too inherent in the basic architecture to be resolved.

Too harsh an evaluation should not be made of CASSM, for it does provide a very good example of the multiple processor direct-search type of data base computer. It was one of the first, if not the first, attempt to construct a special architecture for general nonnumeric processing. Also, it was designed as a research vehicle, not as a commercial product, and perhaps most important, this research is still continuing. Some of the areas either ignored in the description or identified as problems are only now receiving the research attention that is necessary. This is particularly true of both the backup and recovery and the data integrity areas.

Example Data Base and Transactions

CASSM is primarily a research vehicle; therefore, a full DBMS has not yet been developed for it. The following descriptions of transaction processing with CASSM include some extensions to those features currently described in the CASSM literature in order to illustrate how CASSM could function if it were a complete data base computer. In all the example transactions, the conventional CODASYL data base has been used because CASSM is designed for processing hierarchical data structures.

List the address of customer *ABC*.

In response to this query, the host passes the request to CASSM, which results in the loading of either a program or simply a set of parameters and the activation of another program already stored on CASSM. The search, in this case, involves three attribute names and two values. Two of the attributes are for qualification (file name equals customer and customer identifier equals *ABC*) and one is for specification or output (address). Depending on how the record is designed, this query can be processed in one or two revolutions.

Every transaction on CASSM has two data parts: an S part for specifying the data to be retrieved or written and a Q part specifying the qualification that must be met for a record to be selected. The simplest approach is to move forward from the qualification to the specification part of the query. The following is the normal sequence of steps in processing this query. First, the delimiter word is checked for the record to select the proper record type. Second, a search is made for the customer identifier attribute name and the value *ABC*. If this condition is also met, then the record is qualified and the Q bit is set. Next, the remaining attribute names are searched to find the S field (address). Finally, the S attribute name is encountered and the value is retrieved. This case, where the Q fields are encountered first and the record is then qualified before the S fields are read, is called *forward marking*. In general, the Q and S fields can be any distance apart, even at different levels in the hierarchy, as will be seen in some of the later example transactions.

Reversing the order, that is, encountering the S fields before the Q fields, is called *backward marking*. By knowing the relative (not necessarily the absolute) position of the fields within the record, the system can determine whether forward or backward marking will be used and can establish the necessary CASSM instructions. Backward marking uses a one–bit–wide RAM and requires a second revolution to process the query.

As an illustration of the use of backward marking, this type of query is reversed: "List the identifiers for all Minnesota customers." Now when CASSM scans the customer records, the S field is encountered first. This field's relative address on the track is temporarily saved in the RB register. The Q field is found further along in the record and checked. If the record does not qualify, no other action is taken for this record, thereby permitting the RB register to be reloaded with the relative address of the next S field when it is encountered. If, on the other hand, the record does qualify, then the RB register is used as the address of the RAM bit to be set. Thus, on the first revolution, the data base is searched and the appropriate RAM bits are set. On the second revolution, the fields corresponding to the set RAM bits are retrieved (or modified).

The CASSM literature does not explicitly describe how to handle the case where there are several S fields. One possible approach would be to have multiple RB registers and to set RAM bits for all of the S fields when the record qualifies. Then, on the second revolution, all the S fields can be identified solely by using the RAM bits. This approach, however, requires an arbitrary number of RB registers. A second approach, requiring only one register, is to flag only the first S field in a qualified record. Then the succeeding fields in the record can be checked to see if the attribute is one of the S fields.

List the inventory level for part *xyz*.

This query is the same as the previous one, except that a different record type is used.

List all the order numbers for customer *ABC*.

Given the example CODASYL data base design, this query, like the previous two, has both the S and Q fields in the same record (order). Backward marking and two revolutions are required because the Q field (order number) occurs before the S field (customer identifier).

Considering that CASSM is designed for a hierarchical data structure, it should not be surprising that this query and the following one can actually be processed faster and more efficiently if the data base is maintained in a "purer" hierarchical form. Certain fields in the CODASYL data base, that is, keys for the owner records, have been pushed down into the member records. This repetition of keys provides some additional storage flexibility because the members can now be stored anywhere, instead of just following the owner record. However, this results in redundant storage. Moreover, certain queries such as this one require backward marking and an additional revolution for processing. CASSM's natural storage structure, involving linearizing the hierarchy in a preorder sequence, eliminates the need for redundant keys. The extra revolution also can be eliminated by using the forward marking processing technique. Thus, in the CASSM data base, a customer record is followed by all its corresponding order records and not the next customer record. Similarly, each order record is followed by all its item records and not the next order record. On the other hand, inserting new records is more complicated with this structure, as will be seen in the discussion of the add transactions.

Query processing is much simpler if the data base is maintained in this hierarchical structure. The Q field (customer identifier) occurs at one node in the hierarchy. All the subsequent order records have an S field that must be the output response. By the time these order records are encountered, CASSM already knows if they are part of the output response, and thus, only a single revolution is required.

List all the items in order 1234.

This query is the same as the previous one, except that different nodes in the hierarchy are involved.

Reduce the inventory level of part *xyz* by 100.

To process this transaction, each cell scans its data to locate a part record with identifier *xyz*. For every qualified record, the inventory level is then reduced by 100. An important point to note here is that CASSM can process any number of qualified records at the same time. While this allows effective processing of mass updates, it could create a potential problem if only one record were supposed to qualify. The only way to check for this condition is to issue a separate command to count the number of records which qualified before issuing the update.

The basic operation for this transaction is finding the record to update through the use of either forward or backward marking, as with any record retrieval. The update can then be performed in place by CASSM, instead of sending the record to the host. In this specific case, locking is not necessary. In general, however, some method of locking is essential because in some cases, records will have to be sent to the host for further processing to decide whether or not an update is needed or to determine what the new value should be. While the host has the record, it must be locked to prevent subsequent transactions from attempting to modify it. Even if the records can be modified by CASSM, locks are also necessary in those cases where a number of records must all be modified by a single transaction. To date, CASSM researchers have not satisfactorily resolved this issue, so locking on this type of architecture remains an open question. One approach would be simply to set a lock bit in the record.

Add new customer *DEF* to the data base.

The first step in processing this transaction is to check to ensure that the customer identifier *DEF* is unique. This is accomplished by issuing a retrieval request for customer *DEF*. If such a record already exists in the data base, then there is an error because a customer already exists with that identifier. If a record is not found, then the new customer record can be added and it will be unique. This check would be made only if the schema specified that the customer identifier must be unique and either the DBMS or the user on the host issued a specific request to make the check.

The next step is to decide where to place the record. Depending on the implementation, the storage allocation could be performed either by the CASSM controller or by the host. The new record could be placed anywhere in the data base because it is the root of a subtree and does not have a parent node. (A more complicated placement decision is considered in the following transaction.) Over time, the automatic garbage–collection procedures have caused all the garbage words, that is, free space, to migrate to the bottom of the storage for each cell and to the last cell. When adding a record to the data base in this area, any number of words can be added in a single revolution. Therefore, this entire operation requires only two revolutions, one to ensure that the identifier is unique and one to actually write the record. No additional accesses or revolutions are required to set pointers or flags, or to provide other storage overhead information.

Add new order 4567 for customer *ABC*.

This order record can be placed in the data base in either of two ways, but in either case, the initial check to ensure the uniqueness of the order number is the same. The first placement option is similar to the previous

transaction. The order record can be placed anywhere in the free space at
the end of the cell. However, this has an implication for the subsequent
processing and retrieval of the record. Consider the earlier transaction to
retrieve all the order numbers for customer *ABC*. The CODASYL data base
is defined in chapter 3 to include the customer identifier also as part of the
order record. This allows the order record to be associated with the proper
customer record regardless of where it is placed within the data base.
Though greater flexibility for placing the record within the data base is
provided, backward marking and an additional revolution for certain
retrieval operations also are required.

The second alternative is to remove the customer number from the
order record and place the record in the appropriate preorder sequence with
respect to the customer–order–item hierarchy. This requires placing the
record at a specific location with respect to its subtree, although a particular
order does not have to be maintained between subtrees. For example, the
order–item subtrees could be ordered in any way, as long as all the orders
immediately followed their corresponding customer record and preceded
any other customer record. Inserting a record in this manner, however, may
require a much larger block of free space because entire subtrees may have
to be moved to ensure the proper ordering. This operation is actually not
that complex, because any number of words can be added (or moved) in a
single revolution. Thus, with no pointers to update, entire subtrees can be
moved and the new record inserted in the proper location in a single revolution. A benefit of this method is that forward marking can now be used for
certain transactions which previously required an extra revolution and
backward marking.

Which placement method to select depends on the data base design and
the way the DBMS is implemented. While the second method improves the
performance of some retrievals, it results in much greater volatility of the
data base and therefore correspondingly greater backup and recovery
problems.

Add an item to order 1234.

This transaction could be processed in either of the ways described for
the previous transaction.

Delete part *xyz* from the inventory.

This transaction triggers a scan of the data base for the qualified record
(or records). Once the record is found, all the fields within the record are
flagged as garbage words. This action logically deletes the record from the
data base so that a subsequent query would not use it. Dynamically, then,

the garbage–collection hardware physically deletes the flagged words and moves the data words toward the beginning of the track. The effect of this shifting is to cluster all the available space at the end of the track to allow for easy insertions.

When a node is deleted from a hierarchy, there is a question of how to handle the subtree of that node. Frequently, the entire subtree is also deleted. If this were desired, CASSM would simply flag all the words in the entire subtree rather than just the words in the record or node being deleted.

How many open customer orders are there?

CASSM has the capability to perform in hardware certain set or aggregate functions including COUNT, SUM, MAX, and MIN. To process this request, then, each CASSM cell initially sets a counter to zero. Each cell then searches its respective track for order records with no date closed, as indicated by a nonapplicable code. Each time a record qualifies, the counter is incremented. At the end of one revolution, each cell will have built a count of the qualified records that were found. During the time gap at the beginning of the track, the cells send their individual counts to the controller over the bus. The controller will then total the counts from each of the cells to provide a count of the qualified records in the entire data base.

Calculate the total value of all open orders.

This request is processed similarly to the previous one. The date closed field is checked in the order records and the Q bit is set if the record is qualified. When the next field (value) is read, it is sent to an adder, which builds up the total for all the open orders in the cell. Again during the gap, each cell sends its total to the controller, which calculates the grand total for the entire data base. Because of the sequence of the fields in the records, forward marking could be used, so the entire operation can be completed in a single revolution. If the order had been different, backward marking may have been necessary. This would not cause any great difficulty, although it would add an extra revolution to the operation.

What is the average value of the customer orders?

The AVERAGE function is not one of the set functions implemented by CASSM. This function can be performed, however, through a combination of the two previous ones, with the host providing the logic to combine the two results. In response to the previous two queries, CASSM provides the host with both the count and the sum from which to calculate the average. Depending on the actual implementation, this operation could be performed in one revolution if the counter and adder were separate, or in two revolutions if the same piece of hardware performed both functions. Similarly, with duplicate hardware, one or both of these functions could be simultaneously performed on several fields within a qualified record or on records meeting different qualification criteria.

Calculate the total value of the inventory.

This query is the same as the one to calculate the total value of all open orders.

Add 10 percent to the price of item *xyz* for all orders after June 1, 1979.

In this case, all the items in orders after the effective data are checked, and if they do not have the new price, the old price is replaced with the new one. This further results in changing the value of the affected order records.

Several passes are required to process this transaction with the example CODASYL data base. First, the price in the inventory record is changed. Then all the item records are searched to find those records where the date created was later than the effective date of the change and the price was not equal to the new price. These records are then marked for further processing. The unit price is changed, a new extended price is calculated, and the difference in the old and new extended price is determined. This difference is the amount by which the value of the order changed. Ideally, the CASSM hardware is able to make these simple calculations and append a temporary word containing the difference to each item record during a second revolution. If the calculations cannot be performed by CASSM, then the selected item records are sent to the host, where the calculations are performed and the results then written back to the data base. Assuming the records in the data base were stored in hierarchical order, a third revolution is required to backward mark the order records. Several additional revolutions are then required to update the value field in the order records. The exact number of these revolutions depends on both the number of records to be modified and their distribution across the cells.

5-5. Multiple Processor Indirect Search

Approach

The multiple processor indirect search (MPIS) approach is similar to the previous one in that multiple processors are used to process the data base in parallel. The main difference is that the entire data base is not processed in parallel. Instead, a part of the data base is staged onto an intermediate storage device and searched there. This indirect approach is illustrated in figure 5-9.

For this approach to be viable, there must be a way to quickly identify those parts of the data base which must be processed and to load them into the intermediate storage. The former condition requires pointers or indexes to specific parts of the data base. These pointers, though, can involve large blocks of data rather than individual records. For example, it may be sufficient to simply have pointers indicating the tracks or cylinders which contain a particular relation.

The latter condition, rapidly loading the intermediate storage, requires both a high data transfer rate and buffering within the intermediate storage. While the transfer rate of conventional disks is increasing as their density is doubled every 3 years, the size of the data bases is also increasing. A new approach of using parallel transfer disks to read and write multiple tracks on a moving-head disk promises much greater transfer rates.[13]

With the MPIS approach, the time to process a transaction is at least indirectly dependent on the size of the data base. To the extent that the part of the data base that must be searched will fit within the intermediate storage, the processing is independent of the size of the data base. Otherwise, the intermediate storage will have to be loaded and processed several times, and therefore the response time will increase with the size of the data base (or at least the relevant part of it). This increase is not linear, however,

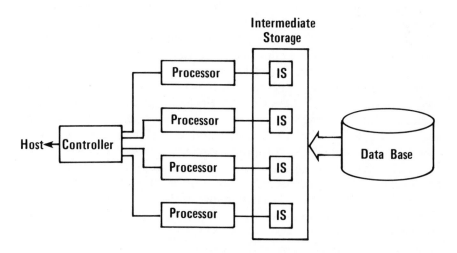

Figure 5-9. Multiple Processor Indirect Search.

because nothing changes until the intermediate storage is filled. At that point, there is a large increase in response time because the intermediate storage must be loaded and processed another time. Loading only a part of the intermediate storage will reduce this time only slightly.

The following two subsections describe the two major systems using the MPIS approach. STARAN, the first system, was developed by Goodyear Aerospace primarily for image-processing applications. It is one of the few systems actually implemented with associative hardware and therefore is a candidate for use in data base processing. In this vein, there has been a joint research program at Rome Air Development Center (RADC) and Syracuse University for several years now on the applicability of STARAN as a data base computer.[14] Most of the discussion of MPISs, however, focuses on the Relational Associative Processor (RAP), a later system designed specifically as a data base computer for relational data bases.

STARAN Architecture

STARAN, the first MPIS data base computer, was originally designed for image processing. Because its basic design is associative, it is also possible to use STARAN for data base management by just changing the software. The software required for the data base management mode, however, is more difficult than on a machine, such as RAP, that was specifically designed for data management.

To operate as a back-end to a larger general-purpose host, STARAN can be connected in any of four ways. Direct memory access (DMA) allows STARAN to read and write directly into the host's main memory similar to an I/O device. A second method is through buffered I/O with most conventional peripherals. A third approach is through external function logic. In this case, a specific memory address is wired so that anything written into that location by one system (either the host or STARAN) is passed to the other system. Each of these methods (including the DMA connection), however, are essentially low-speed communication paths between STARAN and the host. The last and only true high-speed path is with special-purpose parallel I/O transfers directly between STARAN's array memories and mass storage devices. This is also the most expensive approach, however, because this path must be custom tailored for each application or installation. The importance of this parallel high-speed path is apparent, though, when the volume of data that can be moved through the system is considered. Each of the STARAN arrays contains 8K bytes with a maximum of 32 arrays or 256K bytes.

Figure 5-10 is a block diagram illustrating the major components of STARAN. A sequential controller (a PDP-11) controls the internal opera-

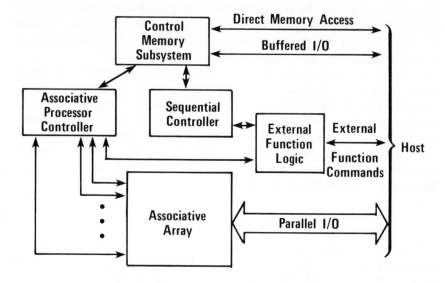

Figure 5-10. STARAN Architecture.

tion of the system and handles communications with the host. A single microcoded associative processor controller controls the operations of the array memories and the associative hardware. Because there is only one set of instruction logic, control, and addressing registers, all the array memories must operate in lock-step, that is, the same instruction is executed at the same time on all of them.

The unique characteristic of STARAN is its 32 associative arrays of 256 by 256 bit memories. Although there is only one set of logic and control registers, each array has a separate word select and search results register with one bit for each of the 256 words in the array. This allows the only exception to lock-step operation in that if a word-select bit is not set during the execution of a particular instruction, then the corresponding word is not processed. A single compare and a single mask register are shared by all the arrays, thus providing a single compare operation in parallel for all the arrays. Any of several relational operations (equal, not equal, less than, greater than or equal, and so on) can be used for these comparisons. Also, all the intermediate storage must be loaded before the search can begin. Therefore, the bandwidth and the time required to load this associative intermediate storage are critical to the system's performance. As an illustration of STARAN's use for data base management, the following queries are considered.

List the order numbers for customer *ABC*.

First, the associative processor controller sets the compare register to customer number *ABC* and the mask register to indicate that only the customer number, not the rest of the record, should be used in the comparison. The arrays are then loaded with the relation linking customers and orders. Because these relations are of fixed length, customer number is always loaded into the same part of STARAN's 256-bit word and therefore is aligned with the appropriate part of the compare and mask registers. The word-select register is next set to ones for all the tuples in the customer-order relation and to zero for all other tuples in the array memories. The comparison is made and a bit is set in the search-results register for every word where a match was found. The search-results register indicates which tuples qualified and should be returned to the user.

List all the engineers in the production department.

In this case, the two necessary comparisons can be performed simultaneously. First, assume that both the job code and the department code occur within the same 32 bytes (256 bits) of the employee record. Then the employee relation, or the necessary part of it, is loaded into the arrays and the word-select bits are set for the appropriate tuples. The result is that there are now ones in two fields of the mask register, the fields corresponding to the job code and the department code. The compare register also has two fields loaded, the job code for engineer and the department code for production. Then, in a single comparison, the query involving the combination of two predicates is resolved and the appropriate bits in the search-results register set.

If the desired part of the employee record is greater than 256 bits, multiple words are required. Each record starts at a word boundary. All the fields to be checked, however, must be in the same 256-bit word. The word-select register is set for only these words, but the entire record is sent to the host.

List all the engineers and accountants.

This type of query requires the Boolean "ORing" of several values for the same item, for example, engineers or accountants. Two comparisons are necessary because only one value can be checked at a time. For this query, then, the registers and arrays are loaded, as in the previous example, to find the engineers. The difference, however, occurs on the second comparison, finding the accountants. For this, only the compare register is changed. The array is already loaded with the employee relation, the mask register specifies the job code, the word-select register specifies which words to check, and the search-results register already indicates some of the desired records. Therefore, the search–results register is not reinitialized or set to an empty state. Following the second comparison, then, it identifies all the records that satisfy either parts of the query.

If the search had required "ANDing" or combining several results, as with checking the range of a value (for example, greater than 0 and less than 10), then for the second or succeeding comparisons, the word–select register would be loaded with the search–results register from the previous comparison. Then only those tuples which met the first test would be used in the second test. In general, any of the basic logical operations can be performed between the search–results register and the word–select register.

Reduce the inventory of part *xyz* by 100.

This transaction is processed in two steps. First, the desired block of inventory records is located and loaded into the array memories. The compare, mask and word–select registers are then set and the comparison is made. The inventory record for part *xyz* is marked in the search–results register. The record and its address are then sent to the host, which actually makes the change and writes the modified record back to the data base. Although some of the isolation, integrity, and security of the data base is reduced by allowing the host to write directly to the data base in this approach, the expensive parallel I/O channel time is not wasted for low data volumes such as single–record updates.

A concurrency problem can arise if both the host and the STARAN are allowed to update the data base. To avoid this problem, STARAN can be used simply as a search device like CAFS, with the host responsible for all the updating of the data base.

RAP Architecture

RAP (Relational Associative Processor) was developed at the University of Toronto in the mid 1970s. Because RAP is not a stand–alone system, a general–purpose host is required to compile high–level user queries into RAP commands, schedule concurrent operations for RAP, and transmit the RAP instructions to the controller. The host is also responsible for all data base integrity and security and for maintaining relation and domain name tables and encode/decode tables. RAP itself consists of a controller, a set function unit (SFU), and a number of cells, each of which is connected to its two adjacent neighbors. The overall RAP architecture is illustrated in figure 5–11.

An individual cell, shown in figure 5–12, consists of an information search and manipulation unit (ISMU), an arithmetic and logical unit

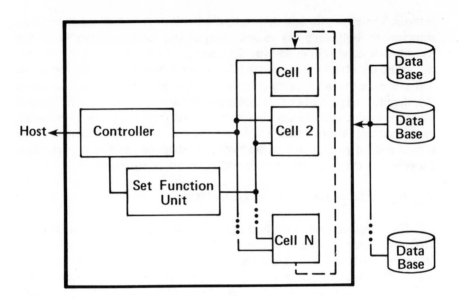

Figure 5-11. RAP Architecture.

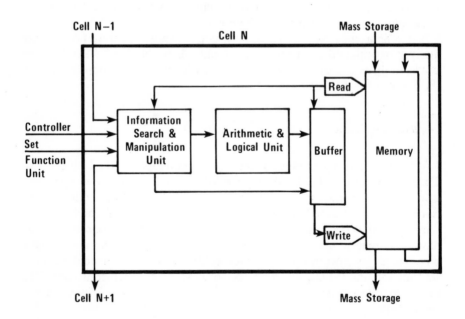

Figure 5-12. RAP Cell Architecture.

(ALU), a buffer, and a memory track. Each cell performs a number of relational operations directly on its own memory or indirectly on the memory of other cells by communicating with its neighboring cells, the SFU, or the controller. The ISMU controls the operation of the cell and provides all its communications with the rest of the system. It also contains one or more (up to a limit determined by the hardware design) selection values, to allow the cell to conduct several searches simultaneously. Because each cell contains its own compare register, lock-step operation is not required.

In operation, the associative store is read into the buffer on each revolution. If the record meets the search criteria, the appropriate mark bits in the data block are set and the record is written out. On a subsequent rotation, all marked records can be retrieved and sent to the host. Therefore, as with CASSM, a complex selection expression can be carried out in a series of steps, with part of this expression evaluated on each revolution.

If the data are to be replaced or arithmetically modified, the operation is performed in the buffer and the modified record within the new value is then written out. If the record is to be deleted, the delete-mark bit is set. The succeeding records are moved up and the deleted record is overwritten at a later time. Garbage collection is thus automatic, with the free space in the associative store clustered at the end of each track.

The controller accepts and decodes commands from the host, loads search criteria into the individual cell ISMUs, and controls the execution of the RAP commands. If certain set functions (SUMMATION, COUNT, MAXIMUM, or MINIMUM) are to be performed on a previously marked set, then the appropriate data are sent to the SFU for integration with the results of all the other cells.

RAP is based on the relational data model, with the data stored in normalized relations. Although a design constraint limits these relations to no more than 101 domains, several relations can be used if more domains are needed. The number of tuples in these relations that are normally stored on a moving-head disk is not limited. If there are too many tuples for a single track, then any number of additional tracks can be used. Neither contiguous tracks nor ordered tuples are required. Only one type of relation can be stored on a single track. If it is necessary to use multiple tracks for a relation, then certain header information must be included on each track.

Two header blocks identify the relation and the domains within that relation. Both relation and domain name are stored as fixed-length codes, with a delimiter code following the last domain name to indicate the end of the list. A physical gap then separates the following data records or tuples from the delimiter.

Each RAP tuple consists of a set of code bits and series of 34-bit-wide data values. The first code bit indicates whether the tuple can be deleted and is used for automatic garbage collection. The next four bits are general-purpose mark bits. If a tuple meets the selection criteria for a query, some combination of the mark bits are set and used by the RAP software, not by any user or application code. The data items following the mark bits can have data values of 8, 16, or 32 bits wide. Each data item consists of a two-bit-length code preceding the 32 data bits. Three of the four possible length codes are used to indicate a quarter-, half-, or full-word (32 bits) data value. The forth code is used to indicate a delimiter block or a track header. These RAP data formats are shown in figure 5-13.

Theoretically, if the RAP data base is small enough, it can be stored completely within the cell memories. In effect, this converts RAP into a direct-search system because staging is not necessary. The more general case, however, is that the data base is too large and must be stored on a conventional moving-head disk. To search a relation, then, the appropriate information is loaded into each cell's intermediate storage. Small relations, those contained within a single track, would be loaded into and processed by a single cell. For larger or multitrack relations, one track would be loaded into a cell and the collection of track information processed in parallel. Very large relations would require this process to be repeated several times.

Intermediate storage within each RAP cell contains the equivalent of

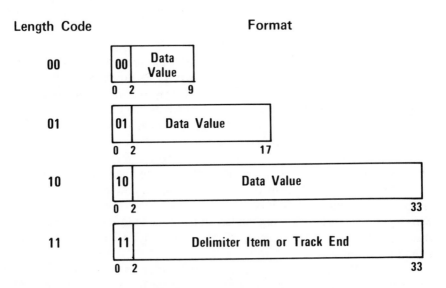

Figure 5-13. RAP Data Formats.

one disk track of rotating memory, for example, disk, bubble, or CCD. In a manner similar to CASSM, the data, rotating through the intermediate storage, are read into the cell's buffer, processed, and written back to the intermediate storage. This particular buffer is 128 bytes long and therefore actually limits the maximum size of a tuple. Thus there are actually two constraints on tuple size, 101 domains and, regardless of the number of domains, 128 bytes.

When a track is read into the intermediate storage buffer, the cell obtains a template of the relation from the track header. Unlike CASSM, where each field is labeled, this fixed–template approach reduces the flexibility of the system because different relations cannot be mixed on a single track. Although some space is saved because a label does not have to be attached to every occurrence of a data item, considerable space on the track is wasted when a relation does not need an entire track. This unused space, though, is available as an overflow area when new tuples are added to the relation, because it is pushed to the end of the track by the garbage collection procedure.

Example Data Base and Transactions

This subsection describes how the typical transactions of chapter 3 would be processed on RAP. Only high–level transactions against the relational and the converted data bases are considered here because RAP is explicitly a relational-oriented system.

List the address of customer *ABC*.

The first step in processing this query on RAP is for the host to locate the customer relation. The current query syntax requires that the user specify the particular relation involved. This is a software design decision, however, and could easily be changed so that if the host knows the required domains, it can determine which relations are needed.

When a required relation is identified and located on mass storage, it is then loaded into the intermediate storage in the individual cells. As the intermediate storage rotates, the entire relation is searched for the tuple with customer identifier *ABC*. When this tuple is found, the address is read and sent to the host. If any additional processing were required, mark bits within the tuple could be set during processing and the modified tuple read from the buffer and written back out to mass storage.

In this example, the mark bit is unnecessary becaue it is as easy to check the customer identifier as the mark bit. The complexity of the selection expression can be defined in relation to the rotational time of the storage.

The mark bit, in this case, effectively converts the complex selection expression into a simple one that is then used for testing in succeeding revolutions.

List the inventory level for part *xyz*.

This query is essentially handled the same as the previous one, except when the inventory is so large that all the tuples cannot fit into the intermediate storage. In that case, the query is processed in two stages. Initially, the first part of the relation is loaded into the intermediate storage and then searched. If the specified part tuple is in this block, the inventory level is read and the processing is completed. If the desired tuple is not in this block, however, then the next block is read and searched. This process is then repeated until either the specified tuple is found and retrieved or the entire relation has been processed because there is no tuple for that part.

List all the order numbers for customer *ABC*.

In either the redesigned relational data base or the converted data base, both the necessary fields, customer number and order number, are part of a single relation. As with the previous examples, the relation customer order in the relational data base or order in the converted data base is located, loaded into the intermediate storage, and searched. Whenever a tuple with the proper customer number is found, its order number is read and sent to the host.

List all the items in order 1234.

As with the previous query, both the required fields for this one are in the same relation. Therefore, the processing is identical, except that a different relation is used.

List all the items in customer *ABC*'s latest order.

This query is more complex because the required fields are not in any one relation. In the relational data base, three relations (customer order, order, and item) must be processed. First, the customer–order relation is loaded and then searched to mark all the tuples for customer *ABC*. Next a "cross–mark" operation is performed between the customer order and the order relations. In the cross–mark operation, if a tuple is marked in the customer–order relation, then any tuple in the order relation with that order number (the common field) is also marked. This is the implicit join operation which RAP has implemented in hardware rather than in software. It is the relational equivalent of a CODASYL user traversing a chained data structure to find all the order records for a given customer.

In the next step, to locate the maximum, or latest date, each cell searches its part of the order relation. For each of the marked tuples, the cell compares its date to the largest one it previously found and saves the larger of the two along with its order number. After each cell has thus processed all its intermediate storage, the results are sent to the set function unit, which selects the largest of the maximums found by each cell. If the relation exceeds the size of the intermediate storage, then this process is repeated until the entire relation is processed.

After the desired order number is so determined, the item relation is searched to find all the items that are a part of that order. Any necessary information about this order can be extracted at this time.

With the converted data base, processing is simpler because the keys have been pushed down to various relations. In this case, the customer number has been pushed down into the order relation. Instead of three, then, only two relations (order and item) need to be searched, thus eliminating the need for the cross-mark operation. With the converted data base, the order relation is loaded, searched, and all the tuples for customer *ABC* are marked. Next, the maximum date is found for the set of marked orders. Finally, this order number is used to mark the desired tuples in the item relation.

Reduce the inventory level of *xyz* by 100.

This transaction makes use of an additional feature of the information search and manipulation unit (ISMU): the ability to modify data as they pass through a cell's buffer. As before, the part relation is located, loaded, and scanned. When the tuple for part *xyz* is found, though, the ISMU does the necessary modification of the inventory-level domain and writes its new value into the buffer. By writing the buffer back to the intermediate storage, the update is completed.

For this transaction, the read, modify and write operations were assumed to be indivisible, thereby removing the possibility of concurrent updates. This is not true, however, if a record is sent to the host for modification before it is returned to RAP storage. The record, in this situation, must be locked to prevent concurrent updates until the host has finished its processing. Locking can be accomplished by simply setting a mark bit indicating that the record is locked. In practice, several mark bits would probably be used to also identify the process that has the record locked. This is important for backup and recovery, because if the process failed, all the records it had locked can be identified, rolled back if necessary, and unlocked by the DBMS during the recovery.

Add new customer *DEF* to the data base.

This is a simple operation in a relational system because the tuples are not ordered. The host locates the customer relation, determines which track has the space for another tuple, and has the cell into which that track is loaded perform the writing of the new customer tuple.

In practice, this transaction requires two steps because the customer number is a unique identifier. First, the customer relation is located, loaded, and searched for a customer with the identifier *DEF*. If such a tuple is found, there has been an error. If a tuple is not found, however, then in the second step, a cell with the needed space is selected and is instructed to write the new customer tuple.

Add new order 4567 for customer *ABC*.

This transaction is similar to the previous one, but with one additional check. The customer relation is first loaded and searched to ensure that customer *ABC* exists in the data base. Then the order relation is checked to ensure that order number 4567 is unique and does not already exist. If so, the add is performed as previously described.

Add an item to order 1234.

This transaction is identical to the previous one, where two relations are tested and an insert is made into one of them. In a CODASYL system, these two operations would be handled differently because the records are at different levels in the data structure and are accessed in different ways.

Delete part *xyz* from the inventory.

This transaction is processed the same for both the relational and the converted data bases. The part relation is loaded, searched, and the tuple for part *xyz* is marked by setting the delete bit. This logical delete is eventually converted into a physical delete by the automatic garbage–collection procedures.

Depending on other data base constraints, some additional processing also may be necessary. For example, a search of the item relation may be made to determine if there are any outstanding orders for that part. If so desired, the order and customer requesting the part could then be listed for some additional action. Similarly, the corresponding tuple or tuples in the part–supplier relation might be identified and deleted. The next step, deleting the suppliers who supplied only the deleted part, might not be performed so as to leave the supplier information in the data base for future transactions.

How many customer orders are there?

Calculate the total value of all orders.

What is the average value of the orders?

Calculate the total value of the inventory.

These four high-level queries are directly implemented in the RAP hardware using the set function unit (SFU). Once the relation is loaded into the cells, a single set function is given and the domain is specified. Each cell then performs this function on all the records in its memory or on the subset with the specified mark bits set. The results from each cell are then sent to the SFU, which combines the results to provide the appropriate overall response. In addition to the COUNT, SUM, and AVERAGE functions used in the preceding queries, RAP also provides two additional functions, MAXIMUM and MINIMUM.

Add 10 percent to the price of item *xyz* for all orders after June 1, 1979.

If there were no effective date restriction with this transaction, the price would be changed only in the inventory record. This involves first locating the inventory relation and then loading it into the intermediate storage. The various cells then scan for the *xyz* tuple, and when found, the ISMU stores a new price equal to 1.1 times the old price. The actual read, multiply, and replace is performed by the ISMU within the cell's buffer, so the entire operation is indivisible, thus eliminating any possible concurrency problem.

By adding an effective date of June 1, 1979, other steps are necessary so that the price can be changed in all the line items for part *xyz* if the order occurred after the effective date of the price change. In this case, the item relation is scanned to locate all the items with part number equal to *xyz* and a creation date later than the effective date. Then the unit price of the item is checked to see if it is the new price. If it still has the old price, then the new unit price must be stored and the extended price must be recalculated by multilying the new unit price by the quantity. While this would be a very complex and time-consuming operation using a low-level CODASYL data manipulation language, it is a relatively simple, straightforward, and fast operation using a high-level relation system.

5-6. Multiple Processor Combined Search

Approach

The multiple processor combined search (MPCS) approach combines several of the best features of both the direct- and indirect-search approaches. With the combined approach, searching is performed on the data loaded into intermediate storage to eliminate the critical time dependencies that arise when the search must be completed in a single revolution of the mass storage device. Also, the multiple processors are assigned to blocks of the intermediate storage rather than directly to every track in the mass store. Therefore, the cost of the system does not escalate drastically with the size of the data base. In addition, the combined approach provides some limited search logic in the path over which the data flow to load the intermediate storage. Simple selection and projection criteria can be used at this point to even reduce the flow of data to the intermediate storage. While the complexity of the operations that can be performed at this point is dependent on the speed of the data flow, arbitrarily complex operations can still be performed in the intermediate storage.

DBC Architecture

Data base computer (DBC), an example of the combined approach developed under Dr. David Hsiao at The Ohio State University, has three major objectives. First, it has to support very large data bases of 10 to a 100 billion characters. Second, it has to support multiple data models, including hierarchical, network, and relational. Third, it has to use current technology and not rely on significant technological breakthroughs. For example, although the design includes some associative memory, the mass storage devices postulate moving-head disk technology.

DBC employs two forms of parallelism. First, an entire cylinder is processed in parallel by a microprocessor associated with each track within the disk cylinder. In CASSM, a microprocessor was provided for each track of a fixed-head disk. Thus DBC's cost is must less sensitive to the size of the data base supported; therefore, very large data bases are feasible.

A second type of parallelism occurs because of the pipeline architecture of the DBC. Because DBC provides a separate unit for each step in the transaction, many transactions can be processed simultaneously. The basic architecture of DBC is shown in figure 5-14 and is explained in the following sections by tracing a query through the system. The possible variations are then shown by tracing an update request.

DBC consists of seven major elements organized into two loops: a structure loop and a data loop. The function of the structure loop is to translate the selection expression in the transaction into physical addresses of the mass storage blocks of data to be searched. These blocks, or minimal addressable units (MAUs) in the mass store containing the actual data records correspond to cylinders on the moving-head disks. The four components in the structure loop are the keyword transformation unit (KXU), the structure memory (SM), the structure memory information processor (SMIP), and the index translation unit (IXU). The keyword transformation

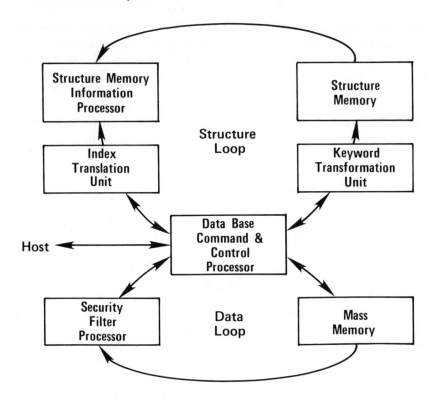

Figure 5-14. DBC Architecture.

unit transforms the request into a series of indexes to the SM. The structure memory, actually an inversion table for the data base, produces logical addresses of the data required to answer the request. The structure memory information processor uses the output of the structure memory to perform Boolean operations on these logical addresses. The index translation unit then translates the logical addresses into physical addresses. Once the appropriate MAUs have been determined, they are accessed in the mass memory to retrieve the specific records that satisfy the request.

User Request. A request to DBC consists of three parts: the operation code, one or more keyword predicates, and the data items to be retrieved or to be modified for an update. The keyword predicates that define the records of interest are logical expressions and as such are either true or false. They consist of a keyword variable name, a relational operator (less than, equal, greater than or equal, and so on), and a value. For example, a query to select all the engineers in the production department has two keyword predicates: skill equals engineer, and department equals production. Depending on how the system is implemented, the request may not need to explicitly specify the file name because the DBMS on DBC can automatically map from a variable name to the file name in some cases. Because the keyword predicate is used by the structure loop to locate blocks of data in the mass storage, the fields in the file which are to be used as keywords must be specified a priori in the data base schema so that the necessary pointers can be built and entered in the structure memory. As with any inverted system, however, all the fields in the file can be used as keywords if necessary.

Data Base Command Control Processor (DBCCP). At the center of DBC is the data base command control processor (DBCCP). The DBCCP receives the user request from the host and converts it into one or more DBC operations. Then, the DBCCP controls each of the other DBC elements as they are used to process the request. Finally, the DBCCP transmits the requested data to the host or acknowledges the update.

Keyword Transformation Unit (KXU). The KXU transforms a single keyword predicate into a form acceptable to the structure memory. Keyword predicates in the form (field name, relational operator, field name), though, cannot be directly processed on DBC but must first be decomposed into a series of basic keyword predicates. All the components of a keyword predicate (file name, field name, and value), except the operator, can be of variable length. All the parts of the keyword predicate, however, are transformed through a set of conversion tables (such as in the example in table 5–1) into fixed–length codes for processing efficiency. Using a simple table lookup, the file name is converted into a fixed–length code. Similarly, another table is used to convert any field in the file that can be used as a keyword into another fixed–length code, which is then concatenated with the file code. A hashing algorithm is used to convert the value in the predicate into a third fixed–length code. Different hashing methods can be used here for different attributes. Finally, the three fixed–length codes are concatenated to provide a single fixed–length code that the structure memory must then locate.

Structure Memory (SM). The fixed–length code generated by the KXU is passed to the SM or the inversion table for the data base. Each entry of the SM consists of a fixed–length code and one or more logical entries, with each logical entry consisting of a logical pointer, a cluster identifier, and a security specification. The SM is then associatively searched to find the entry which corresponds to the code sent from the KXU. This logical entry identifies a logical block of data which may contain records satisfying the keyword predicate. Because several data values may hash to the same fixed–length code, a block may not contain the actual value being sought. The

Table 5–1
Example Encoding Tables

File Table

01   Customer
02   Order
03   Item
04   Part
05   Structure

Domain Table for 01

01   Customer number
02   Customer name
03   Address
04   Credit rating
05   Order number

Domain Table for 02

01   Order number
02   Customer number
03   Customer order set sequence field
04   Ship to address
05   Date of order
06   Date closed
07   Value

corresponding logical block in the mass must nevertheless be searched to locate the desired records.

There is an entry in the SM for each block or MAU which contains qualifying records. If, for example, the records for employees in a particular department are in ten MAUs, then there are ten entries in the structure memory for that particular fixed–length code. An important part of designing the data base for DBC is to appropriately cluster records to minimize the number of blocks searched. This is, therefore, the reason for the second part of the entry, the cluster identifier. When a new record enters the data base, its fixed–length code is calculated and it is placed in a block or MAU as indicated by its cluster identifier.

A difficulty with the cluster identifier is that it can be related to any keyword in the record. This may be resolved through the concept of primary and secondary clustering attributes. No distinction is made if the entire file fits within a single MAU or disk cylinder. If the file spans several MAUs, however, the secondary clustering attributes are used to further partition the file. For example, a company's customer file may span 100 cylinders; ite Chicago customers, 10 cylinders; and its industrial customers in Chicago, only 2 cylinders. With appropriate data base design and clustering, a query involving Chicago industrial customers requires searching only 2 cylinders instead of 100. Because the entries refer to MAUs (that is, disk cylinders) and not to records, both the size of and the maintenance for the SM are reduced. Unlike most inverted systems, however, relatively few queries can be answered using just the inversion table or SM.

The structure memory provides one level of DBC's security. A security atom concept is implemented that provides schema-level security where the user authorization is checked without actually retrieving any data, thus allowing a fast high-level security check. In this concept, each record has a security attribute whose value associates the record with a unique security atom. The user's authorization key then allows access to all the records in a particular security atom, where the records are clustered according to their security requirements. For example, assume that the records which may satisfy a user's request are in three cylinders with three different security atoms. If the user's authorization list only allows access to two of these atoms, the third cylinder is not even scanned. Even though this security-atom approach allows the user to access records in these two cylinders, additional restrictions based on data values also may be present.

Structure Memory Information Processor (SMIP). Individual keyword predicates are transformed by the KXU and then processed by the SM. Most queries, however, involve multiple keyword predicates related by logical operators. For example, a request may contain the multiple predicates (skill equals programmer OR skill equals analyst) or (salary greater than $10,000 AND salary less than $50,000). The SMIP, then, performs the logical operations and combinations on the keyword predicates. For the logical OR case, each block containing records which may satisfy the query must be searched. Because the same block may be identified by both keyword predicates, however, the SMIP can simply eliminate the duplicates and not search the block twice. Thus, once a block has been identified, any additional references to that block are deleted.

The other important function of the SMIP is to perform the more difficult AND operation. In this case, a block or MAU needs to be searched only if it satisfies both keyword predicates or, more generally, all the keyword predicates related by the AND operators. To accomplish this, the first set of MAU identifiers, that is, those which satisfy the first keyword predicate for a request, are loaded into a set of registers in the SMIP and a counter for each register is set to one. After the SM processes the next keywork predicate for the request, another set of MAU identifiers is sent to the SMIP. Each of these new identifiers is then compared with the contents of all the registers. If there is no match, that identifier is simply discarded. If there is a match, however, then the counter for the appropriate register is incremented by one. When all the keyword predicates for the request have been processed, the counters are then tested. If a counter value equals the number of keyword predicates to be "ANDed," then the MAU in the corresponding register may contain a qualified record and must be searched. All the identifiers thus found are then passed to the IXU.

Index Translation Unit (IXU). The IXU accepts the identifiers from the SMIP and converts them from logical to physical pointers. It then passes these physical MAU addresses to the DBCCP, which is responsible for the necessary disk accesses.

Mass Memory (MM). The DBCCP issues a request to the mass memory to access the MAUs or disk cylinders specified by the IXU. With current moving-head disk technology, there is a single access arm on a disk, with one head per track of a single cylinder. Different cylinders are located by simply moving the access arm. Two significant differences distinguish the mass memory from that of conventional moving-head disks. First, conventional disks position in parallel but can read from only one head at a time. With the mass memory, all the tracks in the cylinder are to be read in parallel. Second, the mass memory associates a microprocessor with each read/write head to allow parallel processing of all the data in the cylinder in a single revolution. If extensive processing is required to obtain the qualifying data from the extracted set, then several revolutions may be necessary.

The keyword predicates are sent to the MM, in addition to the KXU, because the actual selection is performed in the MM, whereas the structure loop is used to simply locate the MAUs to be processed. The MM must perform the actual testing of the data to determine the qualified records. Thus, as the records are read, the microprocessors check the actual data values against the keyword predicates and send those records which qualify to the security filter processor.

Security Filter Processor (SFP). The SFP can provide more rigorous security than the security atom specified in the SM which controls access only at the MAU level. Because the SFP examines the actual records that are selected, security checks can be performed at both the data item and data value level. In fact, anything that can be expressed in the complete query language also can be used as a security condition.

A second function of the SFP is to sort records into the order specified by the user. In effect, the SFP receives a parallel stream of records (potentially one from each disk head) and converts them into a serial stream. At this point, then, the SFP can transmit the records to the DBCCP in the proper order within a specific MAU. If the response set includes records in N MAUs, then an N-order merge is necessary to completely order the required records.

There is a significant difference between the MPIS approaches of RAP and RARES[15] and DBC. RAP and RARES currently assume that the entire data base is in the associative store. If this is not the case, then the appropriate part of the data base must be staged into this associative store. The data base is then searched and the desired data are extracted. This approach, therefore, is an attempt to eliminate the index and pointer tables whose use and maintenance result in significant DBMS overhead. On the other hand, DBC attempts to improve DBMS performance by using an associative store for the indexes and pointers so that they can be quickly searched and modified. The data found through use of these pointers are read in large blocks into DBC, thereby reducing the number of disk accesses and also aiding in the performance.

Example Data Base and Transactions

This subsection describes how the example data base and the transactions would be processed on DBC. The discussion is in terms of the redesigned version of the data base. However, in most cases, the transactions are described using both the CODASYL and the relational approach. Table 5-1 is an example of the translation tables that would be used by the keyword transformation unit to convert the search predicates into the necessary fixed-length codes for searching the structure memory. Each file or relation and each field within a relation are identified by a unique code.

List the address of customer *ABC*.

For this simple keyword-predicate query, there is no difference between the CODASYL and the relational version because both approaches would use the customer identifier as the primary key. After receiving this query from the user, the host transmits it to the data base computer control processor, which interprets it and controls its execution on DBC. First, the keyword predicate (customer equals *ABC*) is sent to the keyword transformation unit where it is converted into a fixed-length code. The desired field in this case is in the customer relation which has a code 01 (see table 5-1). The customer number, the field in the keyword predicate, also has a code of 01. To complete this first step, the actual value of the customer number (*ABC*) is hashed to a fixed-length code, for example, *AB* (in which case all customers with identifiers beginning with *AB* are synonyms).

The encoded predicate (0101AB) is then passed to the structure memory, which is associatively searched to locate all the entries with this value. If an entry is not found, then there are no customers whose identifier hashes to the value *AB*, and therefore, customer *ABC* does not exist in the data base. Assuming that there is an entry, though, then there is a record in the structure memory which has the following form

0101AB LB1 CU1 SA1 LB2 CU2 SA2 . . .

The LBs are the logical buckets or MAUs which contain records whose key values hash to the specified fixed code 0101AB. The cluster unit (CU) specifies new record storage, which minimizes the number of MAUs that must be accessed. The security atom (SA) defines the user's access authority to this MAU.

The logical bucket (LB) identifiers are extracted and sent to the structure memory information processor. In this case of a simple single predicate, the SMIP just passes them on to the index translation unit. The logical bucket identifiers are simply the minimal addressable units, that is, disk cylinders, that may contain customer *ABC*. Because all the specified buckets contain customers whose identifier hashes to the fixed–length code *AB*, each of these buckets or cylinders will be scanned to locate the actual record desired. The IXU's function, then, is to convert each of the logical identifiers into the corresponding physical disk cylinder address and to pass the cylinder numbers back to the DBCCP.

In the next stage, the DBCCP positions the disk to read the specified cylinder and sends the actual predicate to the mass memory. As the cylinder is read, parallel track processors scan each track, searching for the customer record with the customer identifier equal to *ABC*. Only the record which qualifies will be selected and sent to the security filter processor, then to the DBCCP, and finally back to the host. The result can then be displayed to the user who issued the request. As was the case with the SMIP, the simple nature of this query does not require any additional processing by the security filter processor. Also, if multiple logical buckets had been identified by the structure memory, then the DBCCP would issue a series of seeks, and the succeeding steps would be repeated for each cylinder.

List the inventory level of part *xyz*.

This query is processed in a similar manner to the previous query. The keyword predicate is converted into a fixed–length code which identifies the part relation, the part number within that relation, and the code for part *xyz*. In this case, if there were too many parts to hash to unique values, a range of part numbers could be hashed to the same code. Once the KXU has performed this transformation, the structure memory is searched to locate the logical cylinders which may contain the part. The IXU converts these logical identifiers into actual physical cylinder addresses and sends them to the DBCCP. The tracks of each of the cylinders are subsequently read and searched in parallel. The desired fields (for example, part number and inventory level) are extracted, passed through the security filter processor, and returned to the user through the DBCCP and host.

The possible size difference in the two files to be searched for the two transactions just described only affects the number of cylinders to be searched. The data base administrator attempts to reduce the number of cylinders to be searched by using various clustering techniques. For example, assume that the firm manufactured both consumer and industrial products, with the latter including both building materials and machine tools. Because it would be very unlikely that an order would include products from all three of these categories, the parts file could be clustered by type of product. Thus the structure memory would specify a different set of cylinders to be searched for the consumer product part number than for an industrial product part number. Because clustering can occur for any number of levels on a single field, for example, part number, consumer products may be further divided and clustered into electronic components and sporting goods for this example. Although each cluster that is maintained will reduce that part of the data base which must be searched to satisfy a query, not too many detailed clusters are needed because the buckets in which the clusters are stored are very large and correspond to entire disk cylinders.

List all the order numbers for customer *ABC*.

With a high-level relational system and the redesigned data base, this query would be processed similarly to the previous two types of queries. The order file is first searched using a keyword predicate of customer equals *ABC*. The fixed-length code is determined using the file name (order), the keyword name (customer), and a hashed form of the value (*ABC*). The structure memory is then entered to locate the logical buckets to be searched. The SMIP eliminates the duplicates, the IXU converts the logical bucket identifiers to physical cylinders, which are then searched, and the results are finally returned to the user.

The low-level CODASYL request, used when only the data base but not the application is converted, is processed differently than the relational type. As described in chapter 3, a conventional CODASYL application on a general-purpose host computer processes this query by first locating the customer record for *ABC*, then locating all the members set of orders for that owner record. This requires one access for the owner record, that is, the customer record, and potentially one access for each of the member records, that is, order records. This is accomplished through a series of requests issued by the CODASYL application program.

With DBC, the application program issues the same set of requests. The first request, to locate the customer record for customer *ABC,* is a simple one-predicate query. Then the application issues a request for the first member of the set of order records for that customer. Unlike the CODASYL system, which uses a pointer in the just located customer record, however, DBC issues a different request to find all the orders for customer *ABC*.

Several points should be noted about the request just issued. First, it is identical to the query of the user of a high-level relational system. Second, the first CODASYL query, to find the customer record, was unnecessary. Third, the request did not ask for the first member of the set, but for all the members of the set of all orders for the customer.

At this point, the query is processed exactly the same as in the relational system. The entire set of records thus found is not returned to the user, however, because the user only requested the first order record in the set; therefore, that is the only record returned. Two additional steps are still necessary and are performed partly within the DBC and partly within the attached host system. The CODASYL user expects to obtain the order records in a particular sequence, for example, by date or size of order. Ideally, this ordering is specified as part of the data base definition, but this is not always the case. Sometimes an implicit ordering exists and is known only to the application program. Although this is not desirable and, in fact, circumvents the intention of a DBMS, it may occur and must be properly handled. Therefore, when the set of order records is retrieved from the mass memory and sent to the security filter processor, the set is sequenced based on the customer-order set sequence field. This sorted set is sent to the host, which then selects the first record of the set and returns it to the user.

The user can obtain the rest of the records in the set through a series of GET NEXT commands. In CODASYL, this corresponds to following the pointer chain to the succeeding members of the set. In DBC, the user continues to issue the series of GET NEXT commands for the succeeding records, but additional access to DBC is not required. The host already has these records and can quickly present the next record in the sorted set to the user.

Thus, when the CODASYL user issues a request for the first member of a set, the entire set is obtained, sorted, and sent to the host. Further references to members of the set require simply accessing a record in the buffer, not another search of the data base. The only additional overhead paid for this anticipatory fetching of the entire set is the sorting done by the security filter processor, which does not affect the overall performance of DBC. This overhead, however, may be unacceptable for high transaction volume, single record direct-access-type applications such as airline reservations. Other techniques or data base designs may be needed to meet the performance objectives for these cases.

List all the items in order 1234.

As a high-level relational query against either the redesigned relational or the converted data base, only the item relation is searched for this query. The structure memory is used to identify all the buckets which may contain qualified item records. These buckets are then scanned and the item records with order number equal to 1234 are retrieved and sent to the host. If an ordering (for example, in order by part number) is required, then the security filter processor sorts the selected tuples in order to return them to the host in the specified order.

In the low-level CODASYL system, which could still be processed, this transaction requires a series of queries, each returning only a single record. First, there is a query of the order relation to obtain the record for order 1234. Then there is a request for the first item record in the set of items in this order. Finally, each succeeding item in the order is obtained using a series of GET NEXT commands.

To process this complete set of CODASYL query requests, which are presented one at a time, DBC first searches the necessary buckets to obtain the record for order 1234 and then sends it to the host. Although this is an unnecessary operation, DBC has no way of knowing this. When the CODASYL query requests the first item record in the set, DBC anticipates a request for all the members of the set and obtains them. The security filter processor sorts the records based on the order–item set sequence field and sends the entire set of records to the DBMS on the host. The host interface for the DBMS then feeds the records to the user one at a time as they are requested.

List all the items in customer *ABC*'s latest order.

The last part of this query is the same as the previous one in which all the items in a specific order were listed. The only difference is that another query is first needed to determine the order number. Thus DBC first scans the order relation and retrieves the order number and date of all orders for customer *ABC*. The security filter processor then orders the records to determine the latest one. This provides the order number for the last half of this query, which is then processed identically to the previous one.

Reduce the inventory level of part *xyz* by 100.

Depending on the software design, this transaction is processed in one of two ways. In the first method, a simple retrieval operation is performed to locate and send the proper inventory record to the host, where the actual modification to the record is made. Then the modified record is written back to the data base. This retrieval operation is the same as the one described for the first two queries, with the exception that the record to be modified is locked. Although, either the DBCCP or the host could lock the record, DBCCP locking is preferred to avoid potential problems in configurations where multiple hosts are connected to a single DBC.

The second approach to this update transaction is to provide a high-level query language to allow the user to specify the complete operations required. Then DBC operates similarly to RAP to read the block of tracks and to make the modification when the proper record is located. In this case, DBC performs all the required operations, thereby eliminating most of the concurrency problems that occur when the host is involved. Although this approach is valid for this particular transaction, in general, update operations may be arbitrarily complex, and this approach may result in problems beyond which DBC is capable of handling. Although DBC reads an entire cylinder in parallel, it writes only one track at a time. This is fine for single–record updates, but updates of a large number of records covering more than one track require one revolution per track modified and therefore are not as efficient.

Once the host has made the change to the records and issued the WRITE command to replace the old value with the new one, the record must again be located. When the record is identified by the track processors, the new record is simply written back to the track instead of the old record being retrieved and sent to the host.

In this case, the modification is relatively simple because the field being modified is not one of the key fields on which the data base is organized. If this is not the case, the old record is first deleted and then a new record with the new key values is added to the data base. This addition is necessary because entries within the structure memory must be changed when key values are changed.

Add new customer *DEF* to the data base.

Although it is not required as part of the add, the add operation would probably be preceded by a retrieval request for customer *DEF*. If the record is found, then there is an error because the customer number must be a unique identifier. In the usual case, a record for *DEF* is not found, and the ADD command is actually issued at this point.

Assume that the customer records are clustered on the customer number, the primary and only clustering attribute. Therefore, the customer records are ordered across those cylinders which contain customer records but are not ordered within a cylinder or MAU. Knowing the customer number, then, a single cylinder or a few cylinders which contain the record, if it is present, or in which the record should be placed, if it is being added, can be identified.

The first step in the add operation is to encode the keyword predicate for the record as if it were being retrieved using its clustering attribute. This involves converting the file name (customer) and the primary clustering attribute name (customer number) to their fixed-length codes and hashing the customer-number value to its fixed-length code.

From this point, the update is processed differently depending on whether or not the hashed fixed-length code is already in the structure memory and space for the new record is available in the same cylinder. If a record with the fixed-length code already exists, then an entry for it was previously entered in the structure memory. Therefore, if the new record can be added to the same cylinder, this cylinder is accessed and the record is added without having to change the structure memory. This simple add is possible because a pointer in the structure memory exists that specifies which cylinder must be searched whenever a request involving that keyword predicate is received.

If either of the conditions (that is, the hashed value is present or space for the record in the same cylinder is available) is not met, then the add operation requires three steps, the last of which may be delayed indefinitely. First, a temporary entry is made in a look-aside buffer once a cylinder has been selected for the record. This entry has the same format as those in the structure memory and will later be integrated into it. The purpose of the look-aside buffer is to allow insertions and keyword value changes to occur immediately, rather than being delayed until the structured memory can be modified. Any time the structure memory is searched, the look-aside buffer is also searched and the cylinders specified by either one are subsequently examined. As soon as the entry has been made in the look-aside buffer, then the data record can be added to the data base. As a result, a retrieval request immediately following the add will successfully find the record, even though the structure memory has not yet been changed. These two steps, creating the entry in the look-aside buffer and adding the record to the data base, are performed immediately. Sometime later, when the system is relatively idle or the look-aside buffer is full, the buffer entries are intergrated into the structure memory and the final step of the add is completed.

Locking is also required in this transaction because the data base is modified, although the method involved has not been completely investigated for DBC. The most desirable approach, however, is to have the DBCCP do the locking so that multiple hosts can share DBC and its data base.

Add new order 4567 for customer *ABC*.

In the simplest case, processing this transaction is almost identical to the previous one. First, there should be a check to ensure the uniqueness of the order number. Next, an entry is made for the record's fixed-length code for the keyword predicate. Space is allocated in one of the cylinders, the appropriate entry is made in the look-aside buffer, and the data record is entered in the mass memory. Later the look-aside buffer entries are integrated into the structure memory.

In practice, this particular add is probably more complex. The preceding description assumes the record has only one keyword, whereas in reality there are probably several, for example, order number, customer number, and date. A fixed-length code entry must be determined and entered in the look-aside buffer for each of these keywords, thus introducing the concept of secondary clustering attributes.

Records are clustered first based on their primary clustering attribute. Then if multiple cylinders are needed, secondary clustering attributes can be used to further reduce the number of cylinders to be searched. For example, assume that the activity against the data base was such that the date was selected as the primary clustering attribute. Further, assume that this reduces the search to ten cylinders. A secondary clustering attribute, such as customer number, can be used to further reduce the number of cylinders to be searched. In this case, the range of customer numbers would be divided into ten segments and an order would be placed in one of the cylinders depending on the customer number. The structure memory would have ten logical entries for the date, one entry for each cylinder that contained records for that date. Among the many more entries for customer number are ten basic entries specifying the range of customer numbers and one logical entry for each date for each of these ranges (assuming that there were approximately the same number of orders each day).

Thus a request for customer *ABC*'s order of June 23 requires searching one cylinder. A request for all June 23 orders for over $10,000 requires searching all ten cylinders for June 23. Finally, a request for all customer *ABC*'s June orders requires searching one cylinder for each day in June.

Add an item to order 1234.

This transaction is processed like the previous one, except that order number would be the primary, and probably the only, clustering attribute.

Delete part *xyz* from the inventory.

The delete operation on DBC is much simpler than the add operation. Although the record is deleted, the structure memory is not normally changed because there are usually many records in the cylinder which hash to the same encoded value. Also, the structure memory still does not need to be changed immediately, even if the last record is deleted. Granted, it would be inefficient to needlessly search a cylinder after the last record that could satisfy the query has been deleted, but the important point is that the query is still answered correctly, even if the structure memory has not yet been updated to reflect the deletion.

The other part of the delete operation involves the actual deletion of the data record in the mass memory. When the DELETE command is executed, the keyword predicates are converted to fixed–length codes and processed as a normal retrieval. The cylinder (or cylinders) which must be scanned is located and accessed. The track processors search their respective tracks for the record to be deleted, in this case, the record for part *xyz*. When this record is found, it is passed to the security filter processor, which checks to ensure that the user requesting the deletion has the proper authorization. This step could be omitted if the authorization does not involve value–based security criteria, although it may be required to ensure the proper author-ization. If the user is authorized to delete the record, then a track processor writes the record back with the delete bit set, the normal, logical DBC delete operation.

If should be noted that the logical deletion operation required two revolutions, one to read and find the record, and one to write the record with the delete bit set. The actual record, however, still has not been physically deleted at this point. Later, during a period of low activity, DBC enters a reclaim or compaction mode. In this mode, the entire cylinder is read, the flagged records are physically deleted, and the remaining records are shifted to fill in the gaps. This physical deletion also requires two revolutions, one to read the records and identify the ones to be deleted, and another to write the compacted data. In principle, all the flagged records in an entire cylinder could be deleted in a single revolution if DBC's design allowed multiple writes. The current design, however, specifies only parallel reads with a single track written on each revolution. This greatly restricts the amount of concurrent updating, although even with this restriction, all the marked records in a track can be deleted in the two revolutions.

How many customer orders are there?

Calculate the total value of all orders.

What is the average value of customer orders?

Calculate the total value of the inventory.

As with most of the data base computer architectures, these high–level commands are processed by the data base computer. With DBC, a command is given to find all the records in the set over which the high–level operation is to be performed. As the set of qualified records is retrieved,

DBC performs the high-level operations of counting, summing, or averaging. Even if the set of records involved spans several cylinders, DBC can build the appropriate cumulative results.

Add 10 percent to the price of item *xyz* for all orders after June 1, 1979.

If there were no effective date associated with this transaction, only the price in the parts record is changed and this transaction is handled similarly to the previous one for changing the inventory level. The cylinder containing part *xyz* is located and searched. The record found for *xyz* is passed through the security filter to ensure that the user requesting the change is so authorized, and then it is written back with the new price on the next revolution. If the price were one of the keywords, this process would be slightly more complex. In that case, the record is deleted and added as a new record with the new price. This approach is necessary to allow the new or modified entries to be created for the structure memory.

This transaction is far more complex with the effective date because it is necessary to change the price not only in the part record, but also in all the item records which have part *xyz* and were for orders after June 1, 1979. From the host's perspective, this transaction is processed with a series of steps very much as if it were using a conventional CODASYL system, although the performance is significantly better. First, the price in the part record is changed, as described previously. Next, a request is made for all the item records with the specified part (*xyz*) that were created after the effective date and that do not already have the new price. Because of DBC's lack of high-level functions, these records are then sent to the host, which recalculates the price and makes the necessary changes in the price and extended price for each item. These modified records are then written back to the data base. The host, though, also must keep a list of all the order numbers in which these items occurred and the change in the value of the order. Finally, a series of change transactions, one for each order, is issued to modify the value of each of the orders for which an item was modified.

The reasons for this complexity are that this transaction requires a series of half or implicit joins to reconstruct the order-item set relation that exists in the CODASYL system, and that part of this operation must be performed on the host. Although this transaction is long and tedious compared with the previous transactions on DBC, it should be remembered that it still requires far fewer accesses and much less pointer following than if it were performed on a CODASYL system using conventional hardware. A final point is that if this type of transaction occurred with any frequency, the data base would probably be designed differently to reduce the number of operations required.

5-7. Comparisons

The previous sections in this chapter identified various types of data base computer architectures and highlighted their features and benefits with specific examples. This section compares these types of systems by applying the evaluation criteria proposed in chapter 4.

The general-purpose back-end data base computer, the usual example of the SPIS architecture, uses a conventional computer architecture and requires a conventional DBMS. Therefore, all the problems of current DBMSs are still present. The opportunities, then, for performance improvement are much fewer with this type of system than with the special-purpose architectures. An extreme example of this type of system is a conventional multiprocessor configuration in which one of the processors is dedicated to the DBMS function. Other things being equal, the performance of the multiprocessor system is actually degraded because the flexibility with which the processors can be assigned to tasks is greatly reduced. The primary, if not the sole, advantage of this type of system is that it is the easiest and least expensive at present to implement because only minimal changes to the DBMS softward and no special hardware are required.

In terms of response time, the MPDS offers the best performance by allowing the entire data base to be searched in one mass storage revolution. This system is currently only effective, however, for small data bases because of its higher storage costs. On the other hand, the MPIS system can handle larger data bases, but its response time is reduced because of the time necessary to load the intermediate storage. Currently, MPIS offers significantly lower storage costs, although the rapidly declining costs of the storage components should reduce this difference. The throughput of these two types of systems, MPDS and MPIS, is difficult to compare without a detailed analysis or a simulation of a specific application.

Backup and recovery are easier, and conventional techniques can be used with an MPIS, where the intermediate storage acts as a conventional buffer. More research is needed, however, to develop backup and recovery methods for the MPDS architecture which involve a continuous read and write operation. In fact, for some MPIS systems, for example, RAP, additional research may also be needed. For all practical purposes, RAP functions as an MPDS system with each cell directly searching its memory once a part of the data base has been loaded into the RAP cells. CAFS, the only current version of SPDS to date, avoids the entire backup and recovery problem by not allowing any on-line updates.

The ease of application development depends more on the level of the data manipulation language than on the type of data base computer architecture, although the ease with which particular language levels can be implemented is a function of the architecture. Currently, the higher-level data manipulation languages are associated with relational systems. Also, these relational systems can be built on a theoretically firmer foundation. All the data base computer architecture types can use the relational data model. Unfortunately, the SPIS, that is, the general-purpose processor, requires extensive storage and processing overhead to support a relational system. All the other architectures can use the relational approach with much less overhead because they are designed to rapidly scan large volumes of data. The undesirability of the SPIS approach is partly due to this difficulty in efficiently and effectively supporting a high-level data manipulation language.

The range criteria include a number of miscellaneous factors, many of which are related. Functional capabilities really involve the ease with which various capabilities can be implemented. In principle, any of the architectures can provide any of the capabilities, although sometimes with prohibitive cost/performance ratios. The SPIS architectures have the same difficulty implementing very powerful, high-level functions as current DBMSs. The only currently available SPDS device is even more restricted in functional capability, since it is limited only to retrieval operations. The most functionality is available in the multiple processor architectures. Each of these can support either a CODASYL or a relational system. The major difference in these basic architectures may be simply a factor of the storage costs, because it is not clear that any of the architectures cannot be designed to provide all the capabilities offered by the others. Unfortunately, this expansion of functional capabilities is not necessarily true for the systems used in this chapter as examples of these three basic architectures, MPDS, MPIS, and MPCS.

Modularity, a family of systems, and fault tolerance form a related set of issues. Modularity suggests that it should be easy to add additional components of a particular type to improve the performance or the tolerance to faults. Although the single-processor architectures obviously offer much less modularity and fault tolerance, a family of single-processor systems can still be obtained by simply replacing the single processor with another more powerful one. Greater modularity and a family of systems can be provided more easily with the MPIS architecture because additional intermediate storage and processors can easily be added. In a more limited case, the intermediate storage blocks can be increased in size or have their access times reduced.

None of the architectures described appear to involve any significant host dependencies, except perhaps the SPIS system. In this case, a natural tendency is to use the same system as both the host and the data base computer.

A high-level interface and a very powerful data manipulation language for a data base computer are very important factors in a distributed configuration because of the associated high communication costs and the long delays. This suggests that the multiple processor architectures, supporting these high-level functions more easily, can provide a more effective data base computer in a distributed system.

The restrictions on the use of a multiple data base computer configuration are caused more by the problems of locking and controlling concurrent updates than by the limitations of any particular architecture. The only effective way multiple data base computers of any type can be used is if the data base can be partitioned so that each data base computer operates in a separate, independent segment. This requires essentially multiple non-interacting data bases. CAFS, the SPDS architecture, is an exception and can be used because CAFS functions solely as a retrieval device and does not perform on-line updates.

Evolvability is the ease with which the data base computer architecture can adapt to changes in either the technology or the data base size and activity. All the improvements in conventional systems, either mainframes or minicomputers, can be directly applied to SPIS systems, though not without some problems. First, all the problems associated with implementing new technology and evolving conventional systems are still present with SPIS. Second, the focus of these improvements is usually on the system's general-purpose performance and might not aid its data base performance.

Improvements in component technology (for example, faster, denser, and less-expensive chips) will improve the performance of all systems. The critical threshold for data base computers has already been surpassed with the availability of semiconductor devices that are small and powerful enough to off-load a significant amount of logic from the host to the storage devices. Improvements in storage technology will allow less-costly storage of and faster access to the data base. Although these improvements will benefit all the architectures, the indirect-search systems, and especially MPIS, will be able to use these storage technologies sooner and at a lower replacement cost. Significant performance improvements can be obtained simply by upgrading the intermediate storage subsystem rather than all the data base storage, similar to improving a system's performance by upgrading only its cache memory rather than all its main memory.

The indirect-search architectures are in a better position to handle the rapidly growing data bases because their data bases are stored on mass storage devices that are less expensive when compared with those of the direct-search systems. For these architectures, only the intermediate storage needs the most advanced technology and the most expensive, highest performance devices. Therefore, as the size of the data base increases, the storage costs do not increase nearly as rapidly as is the case with the direct-search systems. In addition, the performance of these indirect-search systems can be improved by replicating the intermediate storage and the search logic, independent of the size of the data base.

Most of the current associative systems prototypes employ head-per-track disks. Technological developments that led to the current magnetic bubble memory chips and charge-coupled devices (CCDs) have caused the cost per bit of these chips to be comparable with that of a fixed-head disk. Access times, on the other hand, are much faster, approximately 5 ms for fixed-head disk, 1 to 2 ms for bubble devices, and 200 to 400 ms for charge-coupled devices. Future implementations of associative devices on a commercial scale, therefore, would probably use one of these newer technologies rather than fixed-head disks.

Notes

1. E. Babb, "Implementing a Relational Database by Means of a Specialized Hardware," *ACM Transactions on Database Systems* 4, No. 1, March 1979, pp. 1-29.

2. S.Y.W. Su and G.J. Lipovski, "CASSM: A Cellular System for Very Large Data Bases," *Proceedings of the International Conference on Very Large Data Bases,* September 1975, pp. 456-472.

3. P.B. Berra and E. Oliver, "The Role of Associative Array Processors in Data Base Machine Architecture," *Computer* 12, No. 3, March 1979, pp. 53-61.

4. E.A. Ozkarahan, S.A. Schuster, and K.C. Smith, "RAP—An Associative Processor for Data Base Management," *AFIPS Conference Proceedings* 44, 1975 NCC, June 1975, pp. 379-388.

5. J. Banerjee, D.K. Hsiao, and K. Kannan, "DBC—A Database Computer for Very Large Databases," *IEEE Transactions on Computer* C-28, No. 6, June 1979, pp. 414-429.

6. R.S. Rosenthal, "The Data Management Machine, A Classification," *Proceedings of the ACM SIGIR-SIGARCH-SIGMOD Third Workshop on Computer Architecture for Non-Numeric Processing,* May 1977, pp. 35-39.

7. J. Banerjee, R.I. Baum, and D.K. Hsiao, "Concepts and Capabilities of a Database Computer," *ACM Transactions on Database Systems* 3, No. 4, December 1978, pp. 347-384.

8. T. Marill and D. Stern, "The Datacomputer—A Network Data Utility," *AFIPS Conference Proceedings* 44, 1975 NCC, June 1975, pp. 388-395.

9. Babb, "Implementing a Relational Database."

10. H. Chang, "On Bubble Memories and Relational Data Base,"

Proceedings of the International Conference on Very Large Data Bases, September 1978, pp. 207–229.

11. Su and Lipovski, "CASSM."

12. L. Nguyen, "CASSM Simulation," Master's thesis, Dept. of Electrical Engineering, University of Florida, 1979.

13. Ampex Corporation, *PTD-930x Parallel Transfer Drive*, Product Description 3308829–01, October 1978.

14. G.T. Capraro and P. Bruce Berra. *A Data Base Management Modeling Technique and Special Function Hardware Architecture*, Rome Air Development Center, RADC–TR–79–14, January 1979.

15. C. Lin et al., "The Design of a Rotating Associative Memory for Relational Database Applications," *ACM Transactions on Database Systems* 1, No. 1, March 1976, pp. 53–65.

6 Conclusions

Propelled by the rapidly declining cost of hardware, the 1980s will be marked by the ever-increasing use of special-purpose computing devices. To the communication processors, array processors, and fast-fourier transform hardware of the 1970s, data base computers will be added. Through the use of parallel processing, associative addressing, faster components, and hardware dedicated to data base management tasks, data base computers will offer the performance improvements necessary to handle the large volumes of data that are expected in the next few years. Among the other benefits identified for these data base machines are improved cost/performance, the practical realization of the relational data model, and improved data integrity, security, availability, reliability, and maintainability.

This book described the concept of data base management and identified the requirements for the future. Data base computers were postulated as a necessary ingredient in meeting those requirements. Since many data base computer architectures have been and will continue to be proposed, the essence of this book is a logical means for comparing and evaluating these special-purpose designs. Evaluation criteria along with example data bases were described and applied to representatives of the main architectural approaches to date. The advantages and drawbacks of these currently proposed machines were listed and should be useful to designers of the next generation of data base computers. Finally, by illustrating the operation in a typical application environment, potential purchasers and users of data base computers will know what capabilities to demand in these machines and will have the knowledge to use them effectively.

The data base computers described in this book were all in the form of "back-end" devices attached to general-purpose host computers. As such, these data management machines offer a variety of benefits to a broadly based user community. There are some areas, however, where different techniques or devices must be developed because of the data base size, the response time required, or the cost of the data base computer.

A recent survey found that the average data base in the sample was in the range of 600 to 1,000 megabytes.[1] It is anticipated that in the next few years, many users will have data bases in the 10 to 50 billion byte range. Although some of the proposed data base computer designs are modular and can expand to handle increasingly larger data bases, all of them have some practical limit. The apparent solution to this problem is to configure multiple data base computers in such a way as to be able to handle these very large data bases. In order to use these multiple DBCs, however, many of the problems that distributed data processing system designers are encountering must first be solved. For example, if a data base directory exists, where does this information reside? Using the general–purpose host for directory searches is contradictory to the whole data base computer approach. Load sharing, multiple copies for faster access, concurrent updates, and copy management are all potential hazards in the multiple data base computer configurations.

While data base computers will improve the performance of the typical data base management system application, there are some applications that will not be helped. Especially critical are the response times for single–record, direct–access transactions in an intensely active environment such as airline reservations. In fact, many of the airline reservation programs today do not even use the DBMS because of the overhead involved. A restructuring of the data base and programs for this type of application might help somewhat. Actually, what may be needed are data base computers specifically designed for certain classes of applications. More processing power might then be added to perform certain specific tasks, while other logic may be reduced to keep costs in line. ICL's CAFS might be considered as an example of a specialized data base computer for a directory assistance application.[2] Multiple tests may be performed in CAFS against retrieval records, but no on–line updating is provided. Thus the design and use of specialized data base computers is certainly another area for research.

Not everyone who has a need for data management has a large–scale computer system to which a data base computer can be attached. For those with minicomputers or even those without a computer at present, the cost of a data base computer is of prime importance. For both of these cases, a stand–alone version may be the solution. Either the minicomputer could be incorporated into a data base computer design or additional logic could be incorporated into the control portion to handle such tasks as communication with the end user. In either case, the goal is to provide a low–cost facility.

One means of reducing data base computer costs would be to drop the requirements, and corresponding software and hardware, to support existing data models for these stand–alone systems. This should not be a serious problem considering all the new applications and environments for such a device. Reducing the capacity of the mass storage devices associated with these stand–along DBCs also would result in lower costs. For this situation, networks of data base computers could be constructed to share information as well as to obtain information for the data base. Distributed processing type problems, though also would exist here.

Multiple data base configurations, specialized data base computers, and stand-alone versions are all topics for further research. This chapter concludes with the description of two current research topics and the trends associated with them.

6-1. Architecture Trends

The unsuitability of mainframe architectures for data base management tasks has been the impetus behind the special-purpose data base computer architectures. The designs of these devices suggest implementation with a multitude of different logic chips and components. The best performance would be obtained with custom LSI, where the logic design is translated into a unique set of chips. This approach is quite expensive, however, because of the relatively low number of chips that would be used.

Another approach that designers are just learning how to employ effectively in commercial products and which promises to reduce design and manufacturing costs is to use combinations of microprocessors. Sperry Univac in June 1979 announced the 1100/60, the first large-scale general-purpose computer based on bit-sliced microprocessors. This computer was an outgrowth of previous research at Sperry Univac that found that parallel microprocessors can improve performance and reduce manufacturing costs.[3]

The use of microprocessors, especially microprocessors operating in parallel, also can be applied to data base computers. Sperry Univac reported on research in this area at the Fall 1979 IEEE Computer Conference and described one such approach.[4] The parallel transfer of a large amount of data that is processed in parallel on a content-addressable basis by a set of microprocessors is the key to the design shown in figure 6-1.

The architecture of the data base computer shown in figure 6-1 is an extension of DBC.[5] In the original DBC design, two loops were used for processing commands or queries. The structure loop identified the cylinders containing the desired records, performed preliminary security checks, and clustered records to be inserted in the data base. The data loop elements accessed and stored the data base and postprocessed retrieved records. Since the functionality of both the data and structure loops utilize the same parallel processing techniques, this design incorporates both these functions into a single structure.

This data base computer design has six major components:

1. Microprocessor controller (μC).
2. Microprocessor processing elements (μP's).
3. Memory modules (M's).
4. Key processor (KP).

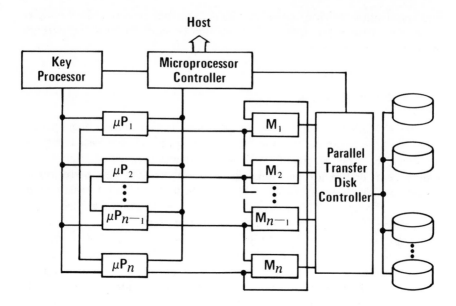

Figure 6-1. Microprocessor–Based Data Base Computer.

5. Parallel transfer disk controller (PTDC).
6. Parallel transfer disks (PTDs).

Depending on the software interface, the microprocessor controller accepts either network data manipulation commands similar to those of the 1978 *CODASYL COBOL Journal of Development*[6] or high–level query-type commands of either a relational nature such as Sequel[7] or a network nature such as QLP 1100.[8] The commands are then processed by the μC, and an appropriate set of parameters and commands is generated for μP's, KP, and/or PTDC operations.

The data base and the directory information that cannot be kept resident are stored on a series of parallel transfer disks. The parallel transfer disk controller handles the transfer of information between the drives and the buffers (M's). The PTDC provides the usual error correction, defect processing, and other features commonly found on disk controllers today. Neither the parallel disks nor the controller involve any technological breakthroughs to achieve parallel transfers. Ampex Corporation has modified one of their 9300 series 300–megabyte disks to offer the transfer of up to nine disk tracks in parallel.[9]

Information from the appropriate parallel transfer disk tracks is transferred simultaneously (that is, in one disk rotation time) into the associated buffers (that is, memory modules). A given memory module has two banks to allow overlap of input and output operations. The memory modules are normally dedicated to a specific microprocessor. They are connected, however, so as to serve two microprocessor processing elements when necessary. The memory modules are sized to contain four disk track's worth of data and at least one half of a disk track's worth of directory or "structured memory"-type of information. For the Ampex PTD with 20 KB per track, the M's would each contain 96 KB of random access memory.

After the memory modules have been loaded with a track's worth of data, the microprocessors start operating on the data asynchronously performing the required functions. The odd and even numbered μP's are connected respectively together via a busing mechanism. This interconnection of these microprocessors and their connection to adjacent memory modules permits operations such as selection, projection, full join, implicit join, addition, modification, deletion, and sort. Data obtained from these operations is subsequently passed back to the host or sent out to the disks.

The key processor (KP) is used to accelerate certain data base operations by providing a temporary partitioning of a file by value. The key processor has been designed to take advantage of VLSI techniques to provide hardware acceleration for the previously listed functions. For example, projection involves selecting only a portion of the qualifying records, which may result in duplicate records. If projection with the elimination of duplicates is desired, the argument string of the qualifying record is presented to KP. If the argument string is already in KP, the record is a duplicate and discarded. Otherwise, the new string is stored in KP and the record is prepared for output to the host or disk.

The modularity of a data base computer constructed from multiple microprocessors lends itself to incorporation over a wide range of system configurations. For large data bases on large mainframes, additional microprocessors could be added to improve performance. For low-cost systems, the microprocessor controller functions may be implemented in software in a minicomputer host. Thus attractive data base computer designs can be implemented with off-the-shelf LSI modules or microprocessors. In addition to allowing flexible configurations to achieve the required performance level, significant cost savings can be obtained over traditional approaches. Therefore, the trend in data base computer design in the 1980s will be to employ these multiple microprocessor devices.

6-2. Data Management Trends

As has been noted throughout this book, most of the data base computers offer the largest performance improvements for arbitrary ad hoc queries for data bases based on "relational" or value-based physical data structures. In chapter 3, a method of converting a network or CODASYL data base to a relational one was described. The CODASYL model, however, is only part of the traditional data management world. Also included are the hierarchical data model and COBOL, FORTRAN, PL/1, and other traditional file system languages. Considering the enormous investment in this current software, a method is needed to handle these too. In addition, to cushion the impact of new data base computer architectures or new data models, the underlying physical data structure should be divorced from the logical data structure.

A method to support multiple data management facilities independently from the physical data structures has recently been developed by Sperry Univac's research organization.[10] Called the *common data base architecture*, this concept is based on the commality of the various languages, data models, and data base architectures. It allows, through a multilevel architecture, the physical data to be defined, accessed, and even administered by any of the current data models or combination of these models. Internally, the architecture of the common data base architecture consists of a physical module and an arbitrary number of identical logical module levels. Data definition and data manipulation are expressed in the common data base architecture by or in terms of a canonical language. User visible data definition and data manipulation constructs, for example, subschemas, queries, or forms are mapped to a single canonical logical schema sublanguage.

The common data base architecture approach to data management is based on transformation between the various data models. Transformation between CODASYL and relational or between hierarchical and relational may be performed either directly or indirectly through transformation to and from a common data model. These transformations may be used to translate the source schema of the CODASYL model to an equivalent schema or subschema of the relational model. In fact, the CODASYL source schema, for example, can be transformed into the storage schema best suited to a particular data base computer.

Many benefits, including reduced costs, improved reliability, compactness, and simplicity, are ascribed to the common data base architecture. This concept is most valuable, though, in providing the impetus toward the unification and simplification of the various approaches to data base systems. With the aid of the data base computers, then, the resulting functionally powerful common data model will allow users in the future to obtain information faster and more easily.

Notes

1. O.H. Bray and H.A. Freeman, "Data Usage and the Data Base Processor," *Proceedings ACM '78,* December 1978, pp. 234-240.

2. *Computer Weekly,* No. 622, October 12, 1978, p. 3.

3. B.R. Borgerson et al., "Mainframe Implementation With Off-the-Shelf LSI Modulels," *Computer* 11, No. 7, July 1978, pp. 42–48.

4. H.A. Freeman, "A Microprocessor–Based Design of the Data Base Computer," *Proceedings of Compcon '79 Fall,* September 1979.

5. J. Banerjee, D.K. Hsiao, and K. Kannan, "DBC—A Database Computer for Very Large Databases," *IEEE Transactions on Computers* C-28, No. 6, June 1979, pp. 414–429.

6. CODASYL COBOL Committee, *CODASYL COBOL Journal of Development*, 1978.

7. D.D. Chamberlain and R.F. Boyce, "Sequel: A Structured English Query Language," *Proceedings of the ACM Workshop on Data Description, Access, and Control*, 1974, pp. 249–264.

8. Sperry Univac, *Query Language Processor* (QLP 1100), UP–8231 Rev. 1, 1977.

9. Ampex Corporation, *PTD-930X Parallel Transfer Drive,* Product Description 3308829-01, October 1978.

10. H.R. Johnson and J.A. Larson, "Data Management for Micro-computers," *Proceedings of Compcon '79 Fall*, September 1979.

Bibliography

Data Base Management Systems

Data Models

Astrahan, M.M. et al. "System R: A Relational Data Base Management System," *Compcon '79 Spring Digest of Papers*, February 1979, pp. 72–76.

Astrahan, M.M., et al. "System R: A Relational Database Management System," *Computer* 12, No. 5, 1979, pp. 42–48.

Astrahan, M.M., et al. "System R: Relational Approach to Database Management," *ACM Transactions on Data Base Systems* 1, No. 2, 1976, pp. 97–137.

Blasgen, M.W., and K.P. Eswaran. "Storage and Access in Relational Data Bases," *IBM Systems Journal* 16, No. 4, 1977, pp. 363–377.

Borkin, Sheldon A. "Data Model Equivalence," *MIT Technical Report*, ILP 2-28-79, 1979.

Chamberlin, D.D. "Relational Data-Base Management Systems," *ACM Computing Surveys* 8, No. 1, March 1976, pp. 43–66.

CODASYL COBOL Committee. *CODASYL COBOL Journal of Development*, 1978.

Codd, E.F. "A Relational Model of Data of Large Shared Data Banks," *Communications of the ACM* 13, No. 6, June 1970, pp. 377–387.

Codd, E.F. "Extending the Data Base Relational Model," *ACM Transactions in Database Systems* (forthcoming).

Codd, E.F. "Normalized Data Base Structure: A Brief Tutorial," *Proceedings of the 1971 ACM-SIGFIDET Workshop in Data Description, Access, and Control,* November 1971, pp. 1–17.

Codd, E.F. "Relational Completeness of Data Base Sublanguages," in *Courant Computer Science Symposia 6: Data Base Systems.* Englewood Cliff, N.J.: Prentice-Hall, 1971, pp. 65–98.

Conference of Data Systems Languages [CODASYL] Data Base Task Group Report. New York: ACM, April 1971.

Date, C.J. *An Introduction to Database Systems.* Reading Mass.: Addison-Wesley, 1975.

Date, C.F. "Relational Data Base Concepts," *Datamation,* April 1976, pp. 50–53.

Fisher, P.S., F.J. Maryanski, J. Slonim, and D.F. Thomure. "Conversion to Relational Data Base Systems: A Case Study," *Kansas State Univ. Technical Report,* KS TR CS 77-25, December 1977.

Fry, J.P., and E.H. Sibley. "Evolution of Data–Base Management Systems," *ACM Computing Surveys* 8, No. 1, March, 1976, pp. 7–42.

IBM. *IMS/VS Programmer's Reference and Operator's Manual*, SH20-9047-0, April 1975.

Johnson, J.R., and J.A. Larson. "Data Management for Microcomputers," *Proceedings of Compcon '79 Fall*, September 1979.

Michaels, A.S., B. Mittman, and C.R. Carlson. "A Comparison of Relational and CODASYL Approaches to Data–Base Management," *ACM Computing Surveys* 8, No. 1, March 1976, pp. 125–151.

Sibley, E.H. "Guest Editor's Introduction: The Development of Data–Base Technology," *ACM Computing Surveys* 8, No. 1, March 1976 pp. 1–5.

Smith, J.M., and P.Y. Chang. "Optimizing the Performance of a Relational Algebra Data Base Interface," *CACM* 18, No. 10, October 1975, pp. 568–579.

Sperry Univac. *Data Management System [DMS 90]*, UP-8366 Rev. 1, 1978.

Sperry Univac. *Data Management System [DMS 1100]*, UP7907 Rev. 3, 1977.

Taylor, R.W., and R.L. Frank. "CODASYL Data–Base Management Systems," *ACM Computing Surveys* 8, No. 1, March 1976, pp. 67–104.

Tsichritizis, D.C., and F.H. Lochovsky. "Hierarchical Data–Base Management," *ACM Computing Surveys* 8, No. 1, March 1976, pp. 105–124.

Zaniolo, C. "Relational Views in a Data Base System—Support for Queries," *IEEE Compsac '77*, 1977, pp. 267–275.

Functions

Batcher, K.E. "Sorting Networks and Their Applications," *AFIPS Conference Proceedings* 32, 1968 SJCC, pp. 307–314.

Bentley, J.L. "Multidimensional Binary System Search Trees in Database Applications," *Carnegie Mellon Univ. Technical Report,* CMU-CS-78-139, September 1978.

Bray, O.H. "Data Management Requirements: Similarity of Memory Management, Database Systems, and Message Processing," *Proceedings of the Workshop on Computer Architecture for Non–numeric Processing*, May 1977, pp. 68–76.

Chamberlin, D.D., and R.F. Boyce. "SEQUEL: A Structured English Query Language," *Proceedings of the ACM Workshop on Data Description, Access, and Control*, 1974, pp. 249–264.

Chamberlin, D.D., et al. "SEQUEL 2: A Unified Approach to Data Definition, Manipulation, and Control," *IEEE Computer Society Repository*, 1978.

Chen, T.C., V.W. Lum, and C. Tung. "The Rebound Sorter: An Efficient Sort Engine for Large Files," *Proceedings of the 4th International Conference on Very Large Data Bases*, 1978, pp. 312–315.

Everest, G.C. "Managing Corporate Data Resources: Objectives and a Conceptual Model of Database Management Systems," Ph.D. Dissertation, Univ. of Pennsylvania, 1974.

Huffman, D.A. "A Method for the Construction of Minimum-Redundancy Codes," *Proceedings of IRE* 40, No. 9, 1952, pp. 1098–1101.

Liou, J.H., and S.B. Yao. "Multi-Dimensional Clustering for Data Base Organizations," *Information Systems* 2, 1977, pp. 187–198.

Lowenthal, E.I. "The Distributed Data Management Function," *AFIPS Conference Proceedings* 43, 1974 NCC.

Moreira, A., C. Pinheiro, and L. D'Elia. "Integrating Data Base Management into Operating Systems—An Access Method Approach," *AFIPS Conference Proceedings* 43, 1974 NCC, pp. 57–62.

Reisner, P., R.F. Boyce, and D.D. Chamberlin. "Human Factors Evaluation of Two Data Base Query Languages—Square and Sequel," *AFIPS Conference Proceedings* 44, 1975 NCC, pp. 447–452.

Rothnie, J.B., and N. Goodman. "An Overview of the Preliminary Design of SDD-1: A System for Distributed Databases," *Proceedings of the 2nd Berkeley Workshop on Distributed Data Management*, 1977, pp. 39–57.

Ruth, S.S., and P.J. Kreutzer. "Data Compression for Large Business Files," *Datamation*, September 1972, pp. 62–66.

Schwartz, Eugene S., and B. Kollick. "Generating a Canonical Prefix Encoding," *CACM* 7, No. 3, March 1964, p. 166.

Sperry Univac, *Query Language Processor [QLP 1100]*, UP-8231 Rev. 1, 1977.

Stonebraker, M.R., E. Wong, and P. Kreps. "The Design and Implementation of INGRES," *ACM Transactions on Database Systems* 1, No. 3, September 1976, pp. 189–222.

Varian Data Machines. *V70 Total Data Base Management System Reference Manual*, 1975.

Wells, M. "File Compression Using Variable-Length Encodings," *Computer Journal*, 15, No. 4, p. 308.

Winterbottom, N. "Integrated Data Dictionary for a Database," *IBM Technical Disclosure Bulletin*, 20, No. 8, January 1978. pp. 3324–3327.

Zloof, M.M. "Query-By-Example," *AFIPS Conference Proceedings* 44, NCC 1975, pp. 431–438.

Zloof, M.M. "Query-By-Example: A Data Base Language," *IBM Systems Journal* 16, No. 4, 1977, pp. 324–343.

Zloof, M.M. "Query-By-Example—Operations on Heirarchical Data Bases," *AFIPS Conference Proceedings* 45, 1976 NCC, pp. 845–453.

Data Base Computers

General

Ampex Corporation. *PTD-930X Parallel Transfer Drive*, Product Description 3308829-01, October 1978.

Anderson, D.R. "Data Base Processor Technology," *AFIPS Conference Proceedings* 45, 1976 NCC, pp. 811-818.

Anderson, G.A., and R.Y. Kain. "A Content-addressed Memory Designed for Data Base Application," *Proceedings of the 1976 International Conference on Parallel Processing*, August 1976, pp. 191-195.

Berra, P.B. "Data Base Machines," *ACM SIGIR* 12, No. 3, Winter 1977, pp. 4-22.

Berra, P.B. "Some Problems in Associative Processing Applications to Data Base Management," *AFIPS Conference Proceedings* 43, 1974, NCC, pp. 1-5.

Bray, O.H., and H.A. Freeman. "Data Usage and the Data Base Processor," *Proceedings of the ACM '78*, December 1978, pp. 234-240.

Bray, O.H., and K.J. Thurber. "What's Happening with Data Base Processors?" *Datamation* 25, No. 1, January 1979, p. 146-156.

Champine, G.A. "Current Trends in Data Base Systems," *Computer* 12, No. 5, May 1979, pp. 27-41.

Champine, G.A. "Four Approaches to a Data Base Computer," *Datamation* 24, No. 12, December 1978, pp. 101-106.

Champine, G.A. "Trends in Data Base Processor Architecture," *Compcon '79 Spring Digest of Papers*, February 1979, pp. 69-71.

Chang, H. "On Bubble Memories and Relational Data Base," *Proceedings of the 4th International Conference on Very Large Data Bases*, September 1978, pp. 207-229.

Coulouris, G.F., J.M. Evans, and R.W. Mitchell. "Towards Content Addressing in Data Bases," *Computer Journal* 15, No. 2, February 1972, pp. 95-98.

Dugan, J.A., R.J. Green, and J. Minker. "A Study of the Utility of Associative Memory Processors," *Proceedings of the ACM National Conference*, 1966, pp. 347-360.

Edelberg, M., and L.R. Schissler. "Intelligent Memory," *AFIPS Conference Proceedings* 45, 1976, NCC, pp. 393-400.

Hsiao, D.K. "Guest Editor's Introduction: Data Base Machines Are Coming, Data Base Machines Are Coming," *Computer* 12, No. 3, March 1979, pp. 7-9.

Hsiao, D.K., and S.E. Madnick. "Database Machine Architecture in the Context of Information Technology Evolution," *Proceedings of the 3rd International Conference on Very Large Data Bases*, 1977, pp. 63-84.

Jino, M., and J.W.S. Liu. "Intelligent Magnetic Bubble Memories," *The Fifth Annual Symposium on Computer Architecture*, April 1978, pp. 166–174.

Langdon, G., Jr. "A Note on Associative Processors for Data Management," *ACM Transactions on Database Systems* 3, No. 2, June 1978, pp. 148–158.

Lipovski, G.J., and S.Y.W. Su. "On Non-Numeric Processors," *Computer Architecture News* 4, No. 1, March 1975, pp. 14–19.

Lowenthal, E.I. "A Survey—The Application of Data Base Management Computers in Distributed Systems," *Proceedings of the 3rd International Conference on Very Large Data Bases*, 1977, pp. 85–92.

Lowenthal, E.I. "Computing Subsystems for the Data Management Function," *Proceedings of the Third Texas Conference on Computing Systems*, November 1974.

Lowenthal, E.I. "Data Base Processors: What Can They Do?" *Computerworld* 13, No. 23, June 4, 1979.

McGregor, D.R., R.G. Thomas, and W.N. Dawson. "High Performance for Database Systems," in *Systems for Large Databases*. Amsterdam: North-Holland, 1976, pp. 103–116.

Minsky, N. "Rotating Storage Devices as Partially Associative Memories," *AFIPS Conference Proceedings* 41, 1972 FJCC, Part 1, pp. 587–596.

Mukhopadhyay, A. "Hardware Algorithms for Non-Numeric Computation," *Proceedings of the Fifth Symposium on Computer Architecture*, April 1978, pp. 8–16.

Rosenthal, R.S. "The Data Management Machine, A Classification," *Proceedings of the ACM SIGIR-SIGARCH-SIGMOD Third Workshop on Computer Architecture for Non-Numeric Processing*, May 1977, pp. 35–39.

Slotnick, D.L. "Logic per Track Devices," in *Advances in Computers*. New York: Academic, 1970, pp. 291–296.

Verity, J. "Data Base Growth Spurs Back-End Unit Evolution," *Electronic News*, March 20, 1978, p. 36.

Yau, S.S. "Associative Processor Architecture—A Survey," *Computing Surveys* 9, No. 1, March 1977, pp. 3–28.

CAFS

Babb, E. "Implementing a Relational Database by Means of a Specialized Hardware," *ACM Transaction on Database Systems* 4, No. 1, March 1979, pp. 1–29.

"CAFS to go on Trial with Directory Inquiries," *Computer Weekly*, No. 622, October 12, 1978, p. 3.

"ICL First with DB Processor," *Computer Weekly*, No. 573, October 27, 1977, p. 1.

CASSM

Bush, G.A., G.J. Lipovski, J.K. Watson, S.Y.W. Su, and S. Ackerman. "Some Implementations of Segment Sequential Functions," *Proceedings of the Computer Architecture Symposium*, 1976, pp. 178-185.

Chen, W.F. "A Performance Study of the CASSM System," master's thesis, Department of Electrical Engineering, Univ. of Florida, 1976.

Copeland, G.P. "A Cellular System for Non-Numeric Processing," Ph.D. dissertation, Department of Electrical Engineering, Univ. of Florida, 1974.

Copeland, G.P., G.J. Lipovski, and S.Y.W. Su. "The Architecture of CASSM: A Cellular System for Non-Numeric Processing," *Proceedings of the 1st Annual Symposium on Computer Architecture*, December 1973, pp. 121-128.

Copeland, G.P., and S.Y.W. Su. "A High-Level Data Sub-Language for a Context-Addressed Segment-Sequential Memory," *Proceedings of the ACM SIGFIDET Workshop on Data Translation, Access, and Control*, May 1974, pp. 265-275.

Healy, L.D. "A Character-Oriented Context-Addressed Segment-Sequential Storage," *Proceedings of the Third Annual Symposium on Computer Architecture*, January 1976, pp. 172-177.

Healy, L. "The Architecture of a Context-Addressed Segment-Sequential Storage," Ph.D. dissertation, Univ. of Florida, 1974.

Healy, L.D., G.J. Lipovski, and K.L. Doty. "The Architecture of a Context-Addressed Segment-Sequential Storage, *AFIPS Conference Proceedings* 41, 1972 FJCC, pp. 691-701.

Lipovski, G.J. "Architectural Features of CASSM: A Context Addressed Segment Sequential Memory," *Proceedings of the Fifth Annual Symposium on Computer Architecture*, April 1978, pp. 31-38.

Nguyen, L. "CASSM Simulator," master's thesis, Department of Electrical Engineering, Univ. of Florida, 1979.

Su, S.Y.W. "Cellular-Logic Devices: Concepts and Applications," *Computer* 12, No. 3, March 1979, pp. 11-25.

Su, S.Y.W., W.F. Chen, and A. Emam. "CASL: CASSM's Assembly Language," *Univ. of Florida Technical Report*, 7778-7, March 21, 1978.

Su, S.Y.W., G.P. Copeland, and G.J. Lipovski. "Retrieval Operations and Data Representations in a Context-Addresed Disc System," *Proceedings of the ACM SIGPLAN and SIGIR Interface Meeting*, November 1973, pp. 144-156.

Su, S.Y.W. and E. Eman. "CASDAL: CASSM's Data Language," *ACM Transactions on Database Systems* 3, No. 1, March 1978, pp. 57–91.

Su, S.Y.W., and G.J. Lipovski. "CASSM: A Cellular System for Very Large Data Bases," *Proceedings of the International Conference on Very Large Data Bases*, September 1975, pp. 456–472.

Su, S.Y.W., L.H. Nguyen, A. Eman, and G.J. Lipovski. "The Architectural Features and Implementation Techniques of the Multicell CASSM," *IEEE Transactions on Computers* C–28, No. 6, June 1979, pp. 430–445.

Watson, J.K., G.J. Lipovski, and S.Y.W. Su. "A Multiple–Head Disk System for Fast Context Addressing for Large Data Bases," *Proceedings of the Workshop in Computer Architecture for Non–Numeric Processing*, 1974.

DBC

Banerjee, J. "Performance Analysis and Design Methodology for Implementing Database Systems in New Database Machines," Ph.D. thesis, The Ohio State University, June 1979.

Banerjee, J., and D.K. Hsiao. "Data Network—A Computer Network of General–Purpose Front–End Computers and Special–Purpose Back–End Data Base Machines," *Proceedings of the International Symposium on Computer Network Protocols*, February 1978, pp. D6–1–D6–12.

Banerjee, J., D.K. Hsiao, and K. Kannan. "DBC—A Database Computer for Very Large Databases," *IEEE Transactions on Computers* C–28, No. 6, June 1979, pp. 414–429.

Banerjee, J., and D.K. Hsiao. "Parallel Bitonic Record Sort—An Effective Algorithm for the Realization of a Post Processor," *The Ohio State Univ. Technical Report*, OSU–CISRC–TR–79–1, March 1979.

Banerjee, J., and D.K. Hsiao. "Performance Study of a Database Machine in Supporting Relational Databases," *Proceedings of the 4th International Conference on Very Large Data Bases*, September 1978, pp. 319–329.

Banerjee, J., and D.K. Hsiao. "The Architecture of a Database Computer. Part I: Concepts and Capabilities," *The Ohio State Univ. Technical Report*, OSU–CISRC–TR–76, September 1976.

Banerjee, J., and D.K. Hsiao. "The Use of a 'Non–Relational' Database Machine for Supporting Relational Databases," *Proceedings of the 5th Annual Workshop on Computer Architecture for Non–Numeric Processing*, August 1978, pp. 91–98.

Banerjee, J., R.I. Baum, and D.K. Hsiao. "Concepts and Capabilities of a Database Computer," *ACM Transactions on Database Systems* 3, No. 4, December 1978, pp. 347–384.

Banerjee, J., D.K. Hsiao, and D.S. Kerr. "DBC Requirements for Supporting Network Databases," *The Ohio State Univ. Technical Report*, OSU-CISRC-TR-77-4, June 1977.

Banerjee, J., D.K. Hsiao, and J. Menon. "The Clustering and Security of a Database Computer," The *Ohio State Univ. Technical Report*, OSU-CISRC-TR-79-2, April 1979.

Baum, R.I., and D.K. Hsiao. "Database Computers—A Step Towards Data Utilities," *IEEE Transactions on Computers* C-25, No. 12. December 1976, pp. 1254–1259.

Baum, R.I., D.K. Hsiao, and K. Kannan. "The Architecture of a Database Computer. Part I: Concepts and Capabilities," The *Ohio State Univ. Technical Report*, OSU-CISRC-TR-76-1, September 1976.

Freeman, H.A. "A Microprocessor-Based Design of the Data Base Computer," *Proceedings of Compcon ' 79 Fall*, September 1979.

Hsiao, D.K., and K. Kannan. "The Architecture of a Database Computer. Part II: The Design of the Structure Memory and Its Related Processors," The *Ohio State Univ. Technical Report*, OSU-CISRC-TR-76-2, October 1976.

Hsiao, D.K., and K. Kannan. "The Architecture of a Database Computer. Part III: The Design of the Mass Memory and its Related Components," The *Ohio State Univ. Technical Report*, OSU-CISRC-TR-76-2, October 1976.

Hsiao, D.K., and K. Kannan. "Simulation Studies of the Database Computer (DBC)," The *Ohio State Univ. Technical Report*, OSU-CISRC-TR-78-1, February 1978.

Hsiao, D.K., K. Kannan, and D.S. Kerr. "Structure Memory Designs for a Database Computer," *Proceedings of the ACM '77 Conference*, November 1977, p. 343–350.

Hsiao, D.K., D.S. Kerr, and F.K. Ng. "DBC Software Requirements for Supporting Hierarchical Databases," The *Ohio State Univ. Technical Report*, OSU-CISRC-TR-77-1, April 1977.

Kannan, K. "The Design of a Mass Memory for a Database Computer," *Proceedings of the Fifth Annual Symposium on Computer Architecture*, April 1978, pp. 44–51.

Kannan, K., D.K. Hsiao, and D.S. Kerr. "A Microprogrammed Keyword Transformation Unit for a Database Computer," *Proceedings of Micro 10*, 1977, pp. 71–79.

Kerr, D.S. "Data Base Machines With Large Content-Addressable Blocks and Structural Information Processors," *Computer* 12, No. 3, March 1979, pp. 64–79.

Manola, F., and D.K. Hsiao. "An Experiment in Database Access Control," *Proceedings of Compsac '77*, pp. 357-363.

RAP

Ozkarahan, E.A. "An Associative Processor for Relational Databases—RAP," Ph.D. thesis, Univ. of Toronto, January 1976.

Ozkarahan, E.A., S.A. Schuster, and K.C. Sevcik. "Performance Evaluation of a Relational Associative Processor," *ACM Transactions on Database Systems*, June 1977, pp. 175-195.

Ozkarahan, E.A., S.A. Schuster, and K.C. Smith. "A Data Base Processor," *Univ. of Toronto Technical Report*, CSRG-43, November 1974.

Ozkarahan, E.A., S.A. Schuster, and K.C. Smith. "RAP—An Associative Processor for Data Base Management," *AFIPS Conference Proceedings* 44, 1975 NCC, June 1975, pp. 379-387.

Ozkarahan, E.A., and K.C. Sevcik. "Analysis of Architectural Features for Enhancing the Performance of a Database Machine," *ACM Transactions on Database Systems* 4, December 1977, pp. 297-316.

Schuster, S.A., H.B. Nguyen, E.A. Ozkarahan, and K.C. Smith. "RAP 2—An Associative Processor for Data Bases," *Proceedings of the Fifth Annual Symposium on Computer Architecture*, April 1978, pp. 52-59.

Schuster, S.A., H.B. Nguyen, E.A. Ozkarahan, and K.C. Smigh. "RAP 2—An Associative Processor for Databases and Its Applications," *IEEE Transactions on Computers* C-28, No. 6, June 1979 pp. 446-458.

Schuster, S.A., E.A. Ozkarahan, and K.C. Smith. "A Virtual Memory System for a Relational Associative Processor," *AFIPS Conference Proceedings* 45, 1976 NCC, June 1976, pp. 855-862.

STARAN

Batcher, K.E. "STARAN Series E," *Proceedings of the 1977 International Conference on Parallel Processing*, August 1977, pp. 140-143.

Berra, P.B., and E. Oliver. "The Role of Associative Array Processors in Data Base Machine Architecture," *Computer* 12, No. 3, March 1979, pp. 53-61.

Caprano, G.T., and P.B. Berra. "A Data Base Management Modeling Technique and Special Function Hardware Architecture," *Rome Air Development Center Technical Report*, RADC-TR-79-14, January 1979.

Davis, E.W. "STARAN Parallel Processor System Software," *AFIPS Conference Proceedings* 43, 1974 NCC, pp. 16-22.

Defiore, C., and P. Berra. "A Data Management System Utilizing an Associative Memory," *AFIPS Conference Proceedings* 42, 1973 NCC, pp. 181–185.

Defiore, C.R., and P.B. Berra. "A Quantitative Analysis of the Utilization of Associative Memories in Data Management," *IEEE Transactions on Computers* C-23, No. 2, 1974, pp. 121–132.

Defiore, C., N. Stillman, and P.B. Berra. "Associative Techniques in the Solution of Data Management Problems," *Proceedings of the ACM National Conference*, 1971, pp. 28–36.

Farnesworth, D.L., C.P. Hoffman, and J.J. Shutt. "Mass Memory Organization Study," *Rome Air Development Center Technical Report*, TR-76-254, September 1976.

Goodyear Aerospace Corporation. *STARAN Reference Manual*, Revision 2, GER-15636B, Akron, Ohio, June 1975.

Oliver, E. "RELACS, An Associative Computer Architecture to Support a Relational Data Model," Ph.D. dissertation, Syracuse University, 1979.

Rudolph, J.A. "A Production Implementation of an Associative Processor: STARAN," *AFIPS Conference Proceedings* 41, 1972 FJCC, Part I, pp. 229–241.

Thurber, K.J., and L.D. Wald. "Associative and Parallel Processors," *Computing Surveys* 7, No. 4, December 1975, pp. 215–255.

Other

Ames, H.C. "RDM—A Relational Database Machine," Lawrence Livermore Laboratory, Univ. of California, Livermore, 1977.

Bird, R.M., J.C. Tu, and R.M. Worthy. "Associative Parallel Processors for Searching Very Large Textual Data Bases," *Proceedings of the Third Non-Numeric Workshop*, May 1977, pp. 8–16.

Canaday, R.W., et al. "A Back-End Computer for Data Base Management," *Communications of the ACM*, 17, No. 10, October 1974, pp. 575–582.

Chang, P.Y. "Parallel Processing and Data Driven Implementation of a Relational Data Base System," *Proceedings of the ACM Annual Conference*, 1976, pp. 314–318.

Copeland, G.P. "String Storage and Searching for Data Base Applications: Implementation on the INDY Backend Kernel," *Proceedings of the Fourth Workshop on Computer Architecture for Non-Numeric Processing* 7, No. 2, August 1978, pp. 8–17.

Cullinane, J., R. Goldman, T. Meurer, and R. Nawara. "Commercial Data Management Processor Study," NTIS AD/A-015790, December 1975.

Dewitt, D.J. "DIRECT—A Multiprocessor Organization for Supporting Relational Data Base Management Systems," *Proceedings of the Fifth Annual Symposium on Computer Architecture*, April 1978, pp. 182–189.

Dewitt, D.J. "DIRECT—A Multiprocessor Organization for Supporting Relational Database Management Systems," *IEEE Transactions on Computers* C-28, No. 6, June 1979, pp. 395–405.

Dyke, R. "Advantage of a Backend Data Base Machine to the Civil Service Commission," *Proceedings of the Third Texas Computer Conference*, 1976.

Eastlake, D.E., III. "Tertiary Memory Access and Performance in the Data-Computer," *Proceedings of the Third Very Large Data Base Conference*, 1977, pp. 259–267.

Heacox, M.C., E.S. Cosley, and J.B. Cohen. "An Experiment in Dedicated Data Management," *Proceedings of the First Very Large Data Base Conference*, 1975, pp. 511–513.

Higbie, L.C. "The OMEN Computers: Associative Array Processors," *Compcon '72 Digest of Papers*, 1972, pp. 287–290.

Hollaar, L.A. "A Design for a List Merging Network," *IEEE Transactions on Computers* C-28, No. 6, June 1979, pp. 406–413.

Holaar, L.A. "Rotating Memory Processors for the Matching of Complex Textual Patterns," *Proceedings of the Fifth Symposium on Computer Architecture*, April 1978, pp. 39–43.

Hollaar, L.A. "Text Retrieval Computers," *Computer* 12, No. 3, March 1979, pp. 40–50.

Hollaar, L.A., and D.C. Roberts. "Current Research into Specialized Processors for Text Information Retrieval," *Proceedings of the 4th International Conference on Very Large Data Bases*, September 1978, pp. 270–279.

Lam, C.Y., and S.E. Madnick. "Infoplex Data Base Computer Architecture—Concepts and Directions," *MIT Technical Report*, CISR No. N010-7808-01, August 1979.

Leilach, H.O., G. Steige, and H.C. Zeidler. "A Search Processor for Data Base Management Systems," *Proceedings of the 4th International Conference on Very Large Data Bases*, September 1978, pp. 280–287.

Lin, C.S. "The Design of a Rotating Associative Relational Store," masters thesis, Univ. of Utah, 1976.

Lin, C.S. "Sorting with Associative Secondary Storage Devices," *AFIPS Conference Proceedings*, 1977 NCC, pp. 691–695.

Lin, C.S., D.C.P. Smith, and J.M. Smith. "The Design of a Rotating Associative Memory for Relational Database Applications," *ACM Transactions on Database Systems* 1, No. 1, March 1976, pp. 53–65.

Linde, R., R. Gates, and T. Peng. "Associative Processor Applications to Real-Time Data Management," *AFIPS Conference Proceedings* 42, 1973 NCC, pp. 187–195.

Love H.H., "An Efficient Associative Processor Using Bulk Storage," *Proceedings of the Sagamore Computer Conference on Parallel Processing*, 1973.

Lowenthal, E.I. "The Backend (Data Base) Computer. Part I and II," *Auerbach (Data Management) Series,* 24–01–04 and 24–01–05, 1976.

Madnick, S.E. "Infoplex–Hierarchical Decomposition of a Large Information Management System Using a Microprocessor Complex," *AFIPS Conference Proceedings* 44, 1975 NCC, pp. 581–586.

Marill, T., and D. Stern. "The Datacomputer—A Network Data Utility," *AFIPS Conference Proceedings* 44, 1975 NCC, June 1975, pp. 388–395.

Maryanski, F.J. "Performance of Multi–Processor Back–End Data Base Systems, *Kansas State Univ. Technical Report*, KSU TR CS 77–07, 1977.

Maryanski, F.J., P.S. Fisher, and V.E. Wallentine. "Evaluation of Conversion to Back–End Data Base Management System," *Proceedings of the ACM' 76*, 1976, pp. 293–297.

Maryanski, F.J., and V.E. Wallentine. "A Simulation Model of a Back–End Data Base Management System," *Kansas State Univ. Technical Report*, KSU TR CS 76–12, 1976.

Moulder, R. "An Implementation of a Data Management System on an Associative Processor," *AFIPS Conference Proceedings* 42, 1973 NCC, pp. 171–176.

Mukhopadhyay, A. "Hardware Algorithms for Nonnumeric Computation," *IEEE Transactions on Computers* C–28, No. 6, June 1979, pp. 384–394.

Operating Systems, Inc. *High–Speed–Text–Search Design Contract Interim Report*, Report 77–002, January 1977.

Parhami, B. "A Highly Parallel Computing System for Information Retrieval," *AFIPS Conference Proceedings* 41, 1972 FJCC, Part II, pp. 681–690.

Parker, J.L. "A Logic per Track Retrieval System," *Proceedings of the IFIP Congress 1971*, pp. A–4–146–A.4–150.

Peebles, R., and E. Manning. "A Computer Architecture for Large (distributed) Data Bases," *Proceedings of the International Conference on Very Large Data Bases* 1, No. 1, September 1975, pp. 405–427.

Rahmer, J., and D. Tusera. "Special Purpose Microprograms and Micromachines for High Speed Information Retrieval," *Technical Report*, IRIA–Laboria, 78150 Le Chesnay, France.

Roberts, D.C., ed. "A Computer System for Text Retrieval: Design Concept Development," Report RD–77–10011, Office of Research and Development, Central Intelligence Agency, Washington, D.C., 1977.

Roberts, D.C. "A Specialized Computer Architecture for Text Retrieval," *Proceedings of the Fourth Non–Numeric Workshop*, August 1978, pp. 51–59.

Rosenthal, R.S. "An Evaluation of a Backend Data Base Management Machine," *Proceedings of the Annual Computer Related Information Systems Symposium*, U.S. Air Force Academy, 1977.

Savitt, D.A., H.H. Love, and R.E. Troop. "ASP: A New Concept in Language and Machine Organization," *AFIPS Conference Proceedings* 31, 1967 SJCC, pp. 87–102.

Savitt, D.A., H.H. Love, and R.E. Troop. "Associative–Storing Processor Study," Defense Document Center, *Document* AD 488538, June 1966.

Smith, D.C.P., and J.M. Smith. "Relational Data Base Machines," *Computer* 12, No. 3, March 1979, pp. 28–38.

Stellhorn, W.H. "An Inverted File Processor For Information Retrieval," *IEEE Transactions on Computers* C–26, No. 12, December 1977, pp. 1258–1267.

Stonebraker, M. "A Distributed Data Base Machine," Univ. of California, Berekley Memorandum No. UCB/ERL M78/23, 1978.

Miscellaneous

Borgerson, B.R., et al. "Mainframe Implementation With Off–The–Shelf LSI Modules," *Computer* 11, No. 7, July 1978, pp. 42–48.

Champine, G.A. "Univac's Financial Model for Computer Development," *Datamation*, February 1977, pp. 53–57.

Flynn, M.J. "Some Computer Organizations and Their Effectiveness," *IEEE Transactions on Computers*, September 1972, pp. 948–960.

Graham, G.S. "Queuing Network Models of Computer System Performance," *Computing Surveys* 10, No. 3, September 1978, pp. 219–224.

Thurber, K.J., and P.C. Patton. *Data Structures and Computer Architecture: Design Issues at the Hardware/Software Interface*. Lexington, Mass.: Lexington Books, D.C. Heath and Co., 1977.

Index

About the Authors

Olin Bray is a principal systems design engineer in advanced systems design at Sperry Univac. He is currently working on data base computer design and performance evaluation, and on distributed data base management systems. Mr. Bray received the B.S. in physics from the University of Alabama, the M.A. and the M.B.A. from the University of Minnesota, where he is a Ph.D. candidate in management information systems. Prior to joining Sperry Univac, Mr. Bray worked on scientific applications, operating systems development, and as the MIS manager for a large health center. Mr. Bray is a member of ACM and DPMA. Mr. Bray is also an ACM national lecturer on data base computers and distributed data base management systems.

Harvey A. Freeman is Manager, Advanced Systems Design, at Sperry Univac. He currently is project manager of Sperry Univac's Data Base Computer Research Project, the objective of which is to determine the feasibility, architecture, performance, and cost–effectiveness of special–purpose hardware for data base processing. Dr. Freeman received the B.S.E.E. from the University of Pennsylvania and M.S. and Ph.D. degrees in electrical engineering from the University of Illinois. Prior to joining Sperry Univac, Dr. Freeman was a member of the engineering staff at RCA, Camden, New Jersey, where he developed models, simulations, and other aids in evaluating data communications systems. During his first years with Sperry Univac, he was in the Defense Systems Division, where he was project engineer for a long–term distributed processing systems research effort and project engineer for the development of an information processing system design methodology. His current research interests are data base systems and local computer networks. Dr. Freeman is also an adjunct professor in the computer science department at the University of Minnesota.